POST CARD

Dear Lord,
Life sure is confusing.
Thanks for always being there,
Bill

HEARTSPRING PUBLISHING · JOPLIN, MISSOURI

Library of Congress Cataloging-in-Publication Data

Putman, Bill, 1942-
  Life sure is confusing / by Bill Putman.
      p. cm.
  ISBN 978-0-89900-950-6 (softback)
  1. Parents—Religious life. 2. Family—Religious aspects—Christianity.
3. Family—Religious life. I. Title.
  BV4529.P88 2006
  248.4—dc22

                                                    2006030208

Dedication

I don't want to leave any "I love you" or
"I'm proud of you" words unsaid.

Jim, God uses your whole life to give me faith in Him. The change in your life, the man you have become, gives me hope that the still broken places in my own life can be changed. When you married Lori to be your wife and our fifth daughter, she brought love, passion, patience, and tenacity to our family. We see the two of you being much better parents than we were. Seeing the way you are raising Christian, Jesse, and Will to attack life and to have a passion for excellence, gives me hope for the future. I see Christ in the way you treat people in ministry. You are indeed, "My son in whom I am well pleased."

Melissa, God uses you to bring me encouragement. God has worked in you, whether it was in a hospital hallway or with a phone call, to help me be stronger. In many ways you are like Barnabas, the "son of encouragement," and so much like Grandma Lois. When you married Mike, and he became our son, he brought humor, a love for people, and loyalty to our family. I see how you are partnering in raising Adam, Zach, and Riley, and I love the way they throw themselves into life. I watch how they treat people, and it brings me great hope for the future. I can paraphrase the words of Philemon 1:4-5, "*I thank my God always, making mention of you in my prayers, because I hear of your love, and of the faith which you have towards the Lord Jesus and toward all the saints.*"

Joni, God uses you in my life to help me to never give up. You remind me of a beach ball in a swimming pool. You can push it under the water, but it just keeps bouncing back. The passion and resiliency with which you throw yourself into your whole life is used by the Lord to help me give my best too. When you brought Jon into our family as your husband and our son, he brought kindness, stability, and an ability to be an anchor. As I watch Ashley and Ethan invade life with excitement and creativity, I can't wait to see how lives will be changed as God uses them. Philemon 1:7 reminds me of you, *"I have come to have much joy and comfort in your love, because my heart has been refreshed through you."*

Angela, God uses your example and love to help me be courageous and willing to sacrifice for my dreams. It seems you have always exploded into life. The infectious way you react to the good and bad of life has affected everyone around you. Your courage to always move forward is such an example to me. When you brought K.C. into our family as our son, I knew that God had sent someone who would love you and bring a balance to your life together. He has the ability to make long-term dreams and has the tenacity to see them through. As I've watched the two of you sacrifice and work towards your dreams, it has encouraged me to persevere with my dreams. As I watch you raise Stephen and Sophia, I can't wait to see what their intelligence and inquisitiveness will bring. To paraphrase 2 Thessalonians 1: 4, *"It is only fitting that I give thanks to God for you, because your faith has grown greatly, and the love you share with each other grows ever larger. Therefore I speak proudly of you because of your perseverance and faith."*

Melody, God uses you in my life to help me be selfless. From a small girl you have had the ability to enter a room and see the hurts of those around you and different ways you might help. God uses you to show all of us how much He cares for us. When you brought Eric into our home to be our son, he brought stability and faith that only comes from time and trials, as well as an ability to be a true friend to all of us. As I watch the two of you team up to raise Jeremy and Jordan, I can see how their gentle love and excitement for life will make a difference in their world. When I think of you, I paraphrase 1 Thessalonians 1:2-3, *"I give thanks to God always for you in my prayers, constantly bearing in mind your work of faith and labor of love and steadfastness of hope in our Lord Jesus Christ in the presence of our God and Father."*

My greatest desire, my most constant prayer is to have 3 John 1:4 be true of my children, their mates, their children, and their grandchildren: *"I have no greater joy than this, to hear of my children walking in Faith."*

My Thanks

- To my wife, my constant friend and companion: I wouldn't want to have lived my life with anyone else.

- To my children: I love you. I'm proud of you. I've done many things in my life that gave me joy and pleasure, but nothing compares to seeing God at work in your lives.

- To my grandchildren: You have given me joy. Your smiles, your hugs, your teasing, and your patience in listening to me. I'm hoping to be there at your weddings and to see my great-grandchildren, but there will be parts of your life I probably won't be here to see. Please love and serve the Lord Jesus and know that I'll be waiting in heaven to welcome you.

- To my extended family: Birth made us related, Christ made us family, and love made us friends. Only God knows the number of times I wouldn't have been able to go on if you hadn't let God use you in my life.

- To my friends: Some people value toys or riches. I value my friends. I am the richest man I know.

- To the churches and ministries I've served: It's OK with me if you forget my name, or what I tried to do, just don't forget Jesus.

- To those who borrowed me for a season as a dad: "Thanks for loving me back." Well, it's time for me to give you my inheritance one chapter at a time.

- To Kristy, Sylvia, Jessica, and others who helped me get these thoughts ready to share.

> From my heart to yours,
> Dad/Grandpa/Bill

Table of Contents

Introduction

I passed out, totaled the car, and could have died. After my mind cleared, I found myself thinking about how close I'd come to going to be with Jesus, and I had mixed emotions about still being here. My daughter Joni asked, "Dad, are there still things you wanted to do that haven't been done yet?"

I said to her, "Let me think about your question."

Here is my conclusion:

I've spent much of my life talking about my own failures or about how the decisions of others have affected my life. I want to spend the rest of my life being honest about the reasons I need God's mercy (what I need, not what I deserve), and sharing with anyone who will listen "what great things the Lord has done for me." Consider the man in Mark 5:1-20. In this passage Jesus tells of a man who's life had been totally destroyed until he met Jesus. When he met Jesus, his life was so changed the Scriptures say, "As Jesus was getting into the boat, the man who had been demon-possessed begged to go with him. Jesus did not let him, but said, 'Go home to your family and tell them how much the Lord has done for you, and how he has had mercy on you'"(Mark 5:18-19, NIV).

So many times I think I've done a better job telling others about the mercy of God to me and of the things God has done for me than I have my own family. Please forgive me. Looking back to my own dad's death I know that his dying left me with unmet longing in my heart. Let me explain.

I've always been lonely for my dad. Many times I've wished that Dad had been able to open his heart and talk to me. When I was young and he was willing to talk, I wasn't willing to listen. When I grew up and wanted to learn from him, I believe he felt so inadequate that he wouldn't, or couldn't, share what he had learned.

Dad entered the hospital for a relatively minor surgery and fell into a coma. Along with my mother, brothers, and sisters, we rushed to be with him, and we waited. Even though the doctor told us we would only wait for him to die, I waited, hoping that he would wake up so I could tell him I loved him. I wanted to have him tell me about his faith in God, that he loved me and was proud of me. But that never happened.

So often I have wished that he had written letters to me, so that when I faced a new crisis in my life, I could go to the place where I store my treasures, take out a letter from him, and read, and reread, the gleanings of his life that would help me with each new difficulty.

Sometime between now and the next thirty years, I'm going to make a trip to heaven, just like my dad, so I thought I'd get ready. As I get prepared for my trip, I've been going through all the things I've valued in my life so I could leave them to those I love most. Farmers leave their land, mechanics their tools, scholars their books, and some people leave their children the wealth that they have acquired. I have to admit, many people would think me a failure. I don't have much money or lands to leave. It seems like I always paid more than it was worth, sold it for less than I paid, or I gave it away.

It seems my life has been a lot like being a miner who works in a whole mountain of rocks and dirt. Every once in a while he finds a precious gold nugget. These little nuggets of gold—or truths, insights, blessings, and answered prayers—have made all the digging in the mountain of rock and dirt worthwhile.

As I look back on my life, I think I've sometimes misunderstood my job description. For instance, I thought I was supposed to fix your problems or heal your hurts, but all the Lord, and you, really wanted was for me to love you unconditionally and be ready to communicate with you, encourage you, and to share what few answers I've learned along the way.

It is my hope that as you will unwrap each of my "gifts," you will carefully consider each of the treasures that have given my life meaning.

A prayer from my journal:

> Lord, it's hard for me to be transparent. I would so much rather be silent about my failures and be well thought of by others. As I write of the times I've needed Your mercy to me, my pride keeps jumping up and saying, "Oh don't say that . . . don't reveal that!"

Father, please remind me all over again that I don't have to be a great person because I have a great God. Please help me remember that You want me to "tell of all the great things You have done for me." Lord, as I write, please help me be real. Father, I thank You that You never left us alone. Thank You for taking our broken home and making it a safe place for my children to come home to. Thank You for healing their hearts and helping me be a dad and shepherd to them. I sure love You, Lord!

Dear Family and Friends

I couldn't wait to be born. If you take a look at me now I think it would be hard for you to believe, but I was born prematurely—weighing only 4 lbs 3 oz. If I had known I would be a broken person born into a broken family who lived in a broken world, I might not have been in such a hurry!

My grandmother on my dad's side was an orphan and didn't know what a healthy family even looked like, so my dad didn't know either. My grandparents on my mom's side really struggled in their marriage and were much better grandparents than they were parents. Bobbi's mom was born to a family of ten children and her dad died at a young age. She stayed at home to help raise her siblings. When Bobbi was just two, her father was unfaithful and her parents divorced. A rejected, brokenhearted woman went back to school and devoted her life to raising her small child.

My own children were born to a dad and mom who really didn't know how to parent. Talk about on-the-job training! Our five children were born in six years to immature parents. We not only didn't know what we were doing, but honestly, often failed to do what we did know to do. We knew how to make babies, but we didn't know how to make a home.

I don't know whether my parents didn't know how to share with me what they had learned along the way, or if

I just wasn't listening as a child and young man, but I entered marriage and fatherhood without a clue. As I look back, I remember my job description being more "worker" at the church and "crisis-manager" at home. I don't want to leave you with a legacy of parenting mistakes, so I thought I'd share what I've found helpful in life!

The subject of this chapter?

There have been so many times I wished my dad had known how to deal with his own feelings of failure and guilt, his feelings of never being able to live up to the expectations life placed on him.

If he had known, had found the answers, I know he would have written the answers to me so when I faced those same crises I would have known what to do.

What do you do when you feel like a failure, guilty, and as if you can't do anything right? What do you do when you can't live up to the expectations imposed on your life? I've tried to find the answers so I'm writing to you.

Thanks for letting me share.
Dad/Grandpa/Bill

CHAPTER ONE

When You Feel Guilty and Want to Start Over

We're All Guilty

A man walked into my office and said, "Bill, I feel so guilty."

I asked him to tell me about his life, and when he finished, I asked, "Do you know why you feel guilty?"

"No" he said.

I smiled and confided, "You feel guilty . . . because you are."

He nodded and hung his head. "So what do I do now?"

How are you dealing with your feelings of guilt? Have the last few chapters of your story, your last days, weeks, months, or years been a tragedy? Do you need our hero Jesus to rescue you? Are you working hard to hide the mistakes you've made from everyone around you—even God? Let there be no doubt, God sees and knows everything and is recording all that we do, think, and say.

- ♦ Revelation 20:11-15: *¹¹And I saw a great white throne, and I saw the one who was sitting on it. The earth and the sky fled from his presence, but they found no place to hide. ¹²I saw the dead, both great and small, standing before God's throne. And the books were opened, including the Book of Life. And the dead were judged according to the things written in the books, according to what they had done. ¹³The sea gave up the dead in it, and death and the grave gave up the dead in them. They were all judged according to their deeds. ¹⁴and death and the grave were thrown into the lake of fire. This is the second death—the lake of fire. ¹⁵and anyone whose name was not found recorded in the Book of Life was thrown into the lake of fire.*

- ♦ Hebrews 4:12-13 (NLT): *¹²For the word of God is full of living power. It is sharper than the sharpest knife, cutting deep into our innermost thoughts and desire. It exposes us for what we really are. ¹³Nothing in all creation can hide from him. Everything is naked and exposed before his eyes. This is the God to whom we must explain all that we have done.*

Are you afraid that your secrets will one day be exposed to everyone? Is your story a great adventure or has it become a tragedy? If your life became a movie, would you want to watch it? It's a scary thought, isn't it? I've thought of it this way. What if the story of my life were to be turned into a movie and shown to my family and friends?

> # Now Showing:
> # The Real Life of Bill Putman!

The first third of my life I thought I was the star of my movie, but it turned out, I was just a supporting actor. I was no hero. In fact, looking back, I was the guy who was in constant trouble, needing to be rescued. I was the one the enemy kidnapped and abused. One minute I was afraid I'd die and the next, I was afraid I'd live! I desperately needed Jesus to come save me!

Let me begin by taking you to 1962, when I was 20 years old. I remember sitting on a rock in Santa Cruz, California, watching the ocean waves pound the shore where people played. My life was already a tragedy. All my dreams were shattered. I had flunked out of college (again), became alienated from the people that meant most to me, and all I felt was hurt, loneliness, and hopelessness. I had finally come to the place where I just couldn't run any more. I hated life and myself and felt like my only options were to either take my life or turn myself over to God to receive my well-deserved punishment. I felt like a guilty man, arrested and standing before the judge and a courtroom full of angry witnesses—all ready to condemn me. This is the picture I could clearly see:

> "All rise!" The accused looks up to see the judge enter the courtroom. All are seated. With his head bowed, the accused hears his name announced and then the prosecutor carefully reads his many offenses . . . and the list of angry witnesses. As he listens to the charges against him, the prosecutor's words cut him like a surgeon's knife, wounding him, revealing his entire miserable life. Even his thoughts and motives are exposed. He listens to the retelling of his childhood and his rebellious teenage years. He had rebelled against his parents, God, and anyone in authority. Finally the witnesses testify to his participation in mischief, sin, and crimes. He knows it's all true; he has failed God, himself, his family, and friends.

> As the prosecutor concludes, the courtroom erupts with the cries from many he's wounded, "He's guilty! Damn his miserable soul!"
>
> The shouts of the angry accusers stop when the judge pounds his gavel and demands silence. He looks down at the accused man and asks him to stand. For just a moment the judge looks into his eyes, and then he speaks, "What defense do you present?"
>
> In almost a whisper the accused says, "I have no defense, Sir. All these things and more are true. I stand here condemned by my own life. I am so sorry. I have no excuse, but please forgive me!" Turning from the judge, he faces the angry people with tears flowing from his eyes. "Please forgive me. If I could live my life over, I would do it so differently." He hangs his head, self-condemned.

That's how I felt. My memories haunted me, like witnesses at a trial, causing me to remember my futile efforts to meet my own needs . . . to get what I wanted. I had tried to fill the hole in my heart with selfish goals, hate, pornography, sex, and shallow friendships. I had surrounded myself with people who were drowning in alcohol and false hopes. I hated myself—an angry man without patience who demanded that others meet his needs—a man who knew what was right but chose to do wrong. I was greedy, filled with hate and envy—a man who lied and used his words to hurt others. I had become a man who completely rejected God, made fun of Christians, and was always disobedient. I could feel myself in God's court of judgment. I had no hope. With so many regrets, so much guilt, I only wished I had a second chance.

Sitting on that rock, watching the waves crash, the weight of my sin overwhelmed me to the place where I was planning my own death. I believe God interrupted my preparation to die as I thought, "Bill, just like the ocean waves have been pounding against the shore, God has been sending His love to you." As difficult as it is for me to understand, or to explain, something wonderful took place that day. Let me try to explain by taking you back to the courtroom.

> Suddenly there's a movement from the back of the courtroom and all eyes turn to see a scarred man approaching the judge. With kind eyes he stops beside the guilty man, and then he speaks to the judge, "Father, I know this man is guilty. Could my death on the cross pay the price for his sins? Would you forgive him and let me help him forgive himself? Would you let me help him seek forgiveness from those he has harmed? Would you let him join me in helping others?"
>
> Hearing these words, angry cries erupt from the witnesses as they shout, "No! Give him what he deserves!"

With the pounding of the gavel, the courtroom becomes silent. The judge looks from his only son to the guilty man. Slowly he raises his voice and proclaims,

"Because of my son, I find this man guilty . . . but forgiven!"

In 1962 the Bill Putman I had become died, and my life began to change forever!

Do You Need a New Start?

I had listened for almost an hour to the story of a brokenhearted man. Eventually he settled back in his chair, ready to listen. I spoke to him about the book his life was writing and I asked him if his book was a great adventure or a tragedy. He said, "It's a tragedy, and I don't know how to change it!"

I reached over and took a book from my shelf and asked, "What if this was the book of your life? How old are you?" He told me he was 43, and I said, "If you live to be 86 years old, your life's book would only be half written. What if you decide to take your life, or you die in an accident today? What would those who love you remember from the last chapters of your life?"

I looked deeply into his eyes and asked, "Rather than quitting, what if you asked God to close this ugly chapter in your book and help you start a new one? If God were to help you start over, what would you like the new chapters of your book to say? What changes do you need God to help you make?"

That man was ready to ask God for a new start. How about you?

Can we really be "Guilty (**of our past**) . . . but forgiven (**in our present**)?" Can our future really be so different from our past? If your life is like a book and each year is a chapter, what if you just keep repeating the failures of your past? When you die, would the last chapters of your book leave you satisfied, or would you die with your dreams still in you?

Consider a popular definition of insanity: Doing the same thing over and over again and expecting a different result. Maybe it's time to let the Lord come into your life and make you a miracle! Jesus came to bring the Good News. You can start over! He wants to be the hero of your story. He wants to declare you,

"Guilty . . . but forgiven!"

My Prayer

Dear Father, I have been the prodigal son and prodigal father. I'm so glad You let me come home to You. I'm so glad You accepted me as You found me: broken, empty, and lost. I'm so grateful You are putting me back together again, and even though I don't deserve it, You have been helping me rebuild a heart and a home for my children and grandchildren to come home to. You have given me true friends. You have used my life to make a difference, and I don't deserve it! But, Lord, I sure do appreciate it. While I'm waiting for my call to heaven, please let me learn not only to believe in You, but to trust You. Please help me not to just act differently, but to be different. Lord, please continue to work in me so when the last chapter of my life is written, my loved ones can see the miracle You've made of my life. I'm glad You love prodigals. I'm glad You love me. Thank You for letting me start over!

Even though I still remember my past (and so does everyone else), the Lord forgave me my past and placed my name in the Book of Life! I'm guilty . . . but forgiven. I'm forgiven . . . and being changed!

Project: Starting a New Chapter

1. Looking back. Ask God to help you see an accurate picture of your life to this point.

2. Ask yourself, "If the next 20 years are a repeat of the last twenty, will my life remain a tragedy or will it become an exciting adventure?"

3. If you are ready for a change, ask Him to help you be "Guilty, but forgiven!"

4. Make a list of what you would like the next chapters to include.

5. Make a list of changes the Lord will need to make in your life so these changes can come true.

6. Pray. Ask the Lord to make a difference in your life one day at a time!

Dear Family and Friends,

One of the crises of life I wish my dad had talked to me about was how hard it is sometimes to understand God. I've often wished he had been able to tell me of how he met Jesus, of his answered prayers, of how he made it through those times when it seems like God doesn't care.

Just so you know, there are times when I look at my past failures or my present problems and I'm not sure God is really there. There have been other times when I believed He was there, but I doubted that He really cared about me.

When I was young, I think I sort of borrowed my grandpa's faith. Over many years of learning that God keeps His word, he trusted God. So, I believed in the God of my grandpa.

I know that you will face many difficult problems in your life, and I wanted to share with you what has helped me when I felt like God wasn't listening.

I love you. If you need to "borrow" my faith for a while, it's okay. I know that the more you get to really know God and His Word, the more you will know He loves you. Then, day by day, difficulty by difficulty, your faith will also grow.

Thanks for reading.
Dad/Grandpa/Bill

CHAPTER TWO

When It Seems Like God Doesn't Care

Where Is God When It Hurts?

There he sits, outside the ICU for hurting families. His family looks more like a train wreck than a family. He watches and waits and prays. His crisis didn't happen overnight. At first he denied his home was in trouble—tried to ignore the growing symptoms. He tried hard to fix the problems. He looked for help in friends, books, seminars, and church, and he talked to anyone who would listen to him. Still he failed over and over again. It's almost like a cloud of doom moved over his life, and now he sits in the waiting room . . . waiting for someone, anyone, to help!

How Are the Pressures in Your Life?

Have you stopped praying that your marriage will be fantastic, and that your children will be healthy, wealthy, and wise and become great spiritual leaders? Are you now just praying that your marriage will survive or that your children will merely stay alive, keep from getting pregnant, stay out of jail, and stay off (or get off) drugs? Are you living in fear that your loved ones are unsaved and that any day an accident could take their lives . . . eternally? Have the problems in your family already destroyed your marriage, or are you afraid your marriage won't survive the next crisis?

Picture yourself in the waiting room for broken families. You're pacing the floors of a hospital waiting room while one of your loved ones undergoes life-threatening surgery. As you wait, minutes tick into hours, hours into days, and days into years, and you are still waiting. Tick, tick, tick; the painful minutes slip by.

In the loneliness of the waiting room, you've tried ignoring the crisis and tried distracting yourself with anything that will take your mind from the pain of waiting. You've listed the things you should be doing, but you've given up trying to do them because you can't keep your mind on other things anyway. You have no words to speak. Your faith needs life support. While you wait, Satan, the accuser of your soul, reminds you of all your past failures, missed opportunities, and words you should (or shouldn't) have spoken. The regrets begin to pile up and you slump in a chair, slipping into despair, self-condemnation, and hopelessness. You withdraw into yourself. Even though there are others you care about in the waiting room, you are so absorbed in your own feelings you cannot see their needs. You know your silence deepens their wounds, but you are weak. Your friends try to say the right words, but their efforts to love you or help you only make you feel more alone in your regret.

Your loved one lies silently in the ICU. Although it pains you to stand by his side, you wait. You want him to wake up, hug you, say, "I love you," and come home. Your only relief is crying out to God.

Where Is God When I Need Him?

I believe God is the all-powerful creator of everything. He is eternal, immortal, all-knowing, ever-present. But in the loneliness of my crisis waiting room, believing hasn't been enough. If my belief doesn't turn to trust, I'm in trouble!

During those desperate times I asked God for help and begged Him to answer my prayers. I've tried bargaining with Him by making promises to Him. I've thought, "If He really loved me, He would come to my rescue!" I've confessed my sin and even made up sins I might have committed to make up for ones I've forgotten. I've hoped and then lost hope waiting for God to show up. I kept calling His Name, but it seemed like He wouldn't answer.

What I Desperately Needed to Learn about God

What I eventually came to understand is that our God, our Heavenly Father, is in the waiting room with us. He's waiting too. As God, He could intervene in our prodigals' lives. He could change their circumstances and protect them from emotional and spiritual train wrecks. He could have kept them from wrong choices and wrong relationships. But because He gave them free will to choose to love Him in return, He's in the waiting room also. Like a Father, He waits. He never forces or imposes. He waits. He waits for them just like He waits for all persons in all places, and if they reject Him, He cries, "How often I would have gathered you like a mother hen gathers her chicks, but you would not" (Matt 23:37 and Luke 13:34).

In story after story, the Bible demonstrates that God, creator, immortal, ever-present and all-powerful, is acting just like a father in the waiting room outside the ICU. In my crisis I panic; in the middle of the crisis, God offers and waits, offers and waits, offers and waits. We may feel like He's not doing anything, but He is. He's just not doing what we want when we want it. He's being God, being consistent, offering and waiting . . . and God knows sometimes it's got to get worse before our prodigal will listen.

Reflecting back, I see that my wife Bobbi and I moved through three stages as we waited in the ICU for hurting families. We finally reached a better understanding of how God loves His children and why He waits.

Stage One—Loving and Wanting Only What Is Best for Your Children

We wanted the best for our children: health, wealth, and happiness. We wanted our children to know and love God, be like Him, and be protected from this world. We wanted them to be productive, to find someone to love them, and then go to heaven when they die. We wanted God's blessing on our family.

Do our hopes for our family sound familiar? God gave Adam and Eve the beautiful Garden of Eden. It was a place without weeds, conflict, or disease. God gave him a partner and helper in Eve. He intimately gave of Himself in His relationship with Adam and Eve. He gave them all of the above and still they rebelled.

Stage Two—Loving and Being Willing to Personally Suffer So Your Children Can Be Saved

When those we love turned from God's best, *we became willing to suffer for them* so they could find forgiveness and eternal life. We grieved that they had turned from God's best, and we became willing to suffer, pay the price for their failure, even die for them, if it meant they could be saved.

Does our desire to rescue our children sound familiar? God did this for each of us. God, the Son, left heaven and took upon Himself the likeness of men and was willing to suffer to meet his children's greatest needs: forgiveness and eternal salvation. He was willing to come live with us, to show us how to live and love. He was willing to die on a cross, taking the punishment of the guilty so the guilty could be forgiven. He chose to lose so we could gain! He offered Himself as a living sacrifice for all who would accept Him. He offered and waited. He still offers and waits.

Stage Three—Loving and Being Willing to Have Your Children Suffer So They Can Be Saved

There came a point when we realized that we were not only willing to suffer so our children could be saved, we were willing for *them to suffer* if it meant they would turn to God. I remember when Bobbi and I prayed, "Lord, whatever it takes." We finally understood that it might be necessary for our loved ones to suffer the loss of health, wealth, happiness, or even long life, in order for them to be saved. We wanted whatever it took to bring them back to God. We tried to stop asking God for what *we* thought was best and asked Him to help us *trust* Him to know what is best. We are learning to trust God to use crisis to bring them to Christ or bring them to maturity.

We've found that sometimes God answers prayers by taking away pressures, but sometimes He doesn't. Sometimes He chooses to let us grow through crisis so we will learn to trust Him. We're learning that God often uses crisis to discipline His children because we have to face the consequences of our choices. God sometimes allows us to suffer so others can be saved. He even allows entire cultures and nations to collapse so the rest of the world will be warned and turn to the Lord.

It Sure Is Confusing!

It's hard: wanting only good for those we love, being willing to suffer so those we love can be saved, and finally praying, "Whatever it takes, Lord!"

Maybe you're thinking, "Okay, looking at these three stages I think I understand, but I still want to protect those I love from pain!" I know that in my family experience, I've often been confused and I have given up hope. Sometimes I don't see His action in my life or in response to my prayers, and I won't until I get to heaven.

In crisis, I find my greatest comfort in knowing that God is right there with me in my ICU waiting room. What He chooses to do will always be right. I will understand it when I get to heaven, or it won't matter to me then . . . but, God *is* God and *I trust Him!*

♦ 2 Corinthians 1:8-9. (NLT): *⁸I think you ought to know, dear friends, about the trouble we went through in the province of Asia. We were crushed and completely overwhelmed, and we thought we would never live through it. ⁹In fact, we expected to die. But as a result, we learned not to rely on ourselves, but on God who can raise the dead.*

Finally, in the middle of my confusion and doubt, when I don't understand, I can believe. But even if I can't believe, I can trust. But even when I can't understand, believe, or trust, God will still be God. He is not limited by my understanding or trust. He will still be the God who loves and offers, who acts like a father waiting with me in the ICU waiting room for wounded families. He waited for me. He waited for you, He is waiting for yours.

I'm trying to trust Him even when I don't understand.

Dear Family and Friends,

My grandfather, Elmer Newton, is one of my heroes. In the first half of his life he served himself, and he failed God, his wife, and his children. But before he died, God used him to help me understand that God gives mercy for our past and can do great things in our future.

The last time I saw him he was 91, had suffered a stroke, and was confined to a wheelchair. As I prepared to say goodbye to him, for what turned out to be the last time, I said, "I love you, Grandpa. If I don't see you again here, I'll see you in heaven!" He looked me in the eye, looked away, and said, "I'm not sure." I said, "Grandpa, are you sitting here remembering the sins of your life, especially the first 50 years?" He whispered, "Yes." I said, "Grandpa, have you asked the Lord to forgive you? Have you accepted Him as your Savior?" He nodded his head and said, "Yes." I then reminded him, "Then Grandpa, you are saved, not because of how good you are, but because of how good He is. He promised to save you, and He will keep His word. Grandpa, if I don't see you again down here, I'll see you in heaven."

When it's my turn to say goodbye to this life and go face God, I may have a stroke and be confined to a wheelchair. Like Grandpa, I may be remembering the ways I let you and the Lord down. Please come see me, and remind me that God will keep His word, will forgive my sin, and take me to heaven. Would you help me remember "it's not how good I am that matters but how good He is"?

I love you, not for what you do or don't do. I love you. I hope you will let the Lord make a miracle of your life. If I don't see you again here on earth, I want to see you in heaven!

Dad / Grandpa / Bill

CHAPTER THREE
When You Can't Forgive Yourself

Starting Over Is a Process of Being Restored

Over the years I've listened to many brokenhearted people. In their own eyes, and maybe even the eyes of those around them, they are "damaged goods" rather than the priceless treasures God intends them to be . . . and they need hope. Do you?

We Can't Go Back, but We Can Start Over

I remember a young girl in one of our first ministries named Lynn. God and her mother had made her beautiful, but her guilt made her ugly. I remember her inability to look anyone in the eye and how she struggled to share her thoughts. She explained how she had tried sex to gain approval and drugs to hide her pain. I remember how she eventually stood beside her best friend, Robbie, and asked Jesus to become her Savior. The youth and I dammed up a little creek, forming a small pond, and I baptized her into Christ. She began a lifelong process of restoration. Now, I don't remember her for the life she led before, but for the lesson she taught me: You can't go back, but because of Jesus Christ, you can start over!

Years later, I remember an anxious mother demanding over the phone, "Get over here. My daughter is pregnant, and I know her father will kill her!" I hurried to their home, arriving just before the father, and heard him ask where his daughter was. With head hung low, she walked out of the bedroom to face her dad. I saw him reach out to her, and, in his own way, he acted just like our Heavenly Father, I watched him reach out to help her start walking through the hurts and beginning the process of restoring her.

When You Look Back and Only See Regret

Have you ever taken a backward look at your life and started playing the "I-wish-I-could-go-back-and- start- over" game?

Looking back, there are so many regrets about my childhood, my teenage years, the things I did and didn't do in the early years of my marriage. As a parent I wish I'd have listened more to my children, been more patient, complimented them more often, and made more time for them. I wish I wouldn't have just prayed *for* them, but *with* them . . . and more often. I wish I had asked their opinions, corrected them in private, and been more loving and kind. If only I had kept my mouth shut when they were distressed and just been a shoulder for them to lean on. I wish I had been more "friend" and less "preacher" when they had a problem. I've often thought regretfully, "If only I had treated them like the treasures they are—with tenderness and compassion. If only I had been more forgiving."

As a husband, I have often lamented, "I wish I had treated her better—told her how much I love her and how precious she is to me. I wish I had remembered to buy my wife flowers for no reason at all or had helped more with the home and children. I wish I had met her sexual needs before satisfying my own." I should have been the first to seek an end to an argument. I should have found out what made her insecure in our relationship and worked hard to remove it. I wish I had shown her more affection in public. The list goes on and on, but I can't go back and "fix it."

If You Can't Go Back, How Do You Start Over?

One day a woman walked into my office and for more than an hour I listened with my whole heart. (Because I want to protect her privacy I've changed the story enough that it could fit many others that have shared their broken hearts with me.) She was an unwanted child. Her parents either could not or would not take care of her, and she was passed around to other family members who really didn't want her. Eventually she became a part of the foster care system. She was sexually abused. As a teenager she was lonely and desperately wanted someone to love her; she became promiscuous. She got pregnant and had an abortion. This poor woman had experienced one broken relationship after another, and although now married, she had decided she just couldn't trust anymore.

She lifted up her hands and showed me her wrists and said, "See the scars? I tried suicide twice. My life is so empty. No matter how much my husband or children or church try to show me love, I still feel so empty." She sobbed, and the tears fell silently from her cheeks. I asked if I could pray with her. I prayed for her broken memories and her broken past, and I asked God to help her. I prayed that He would begin the process of restoration.

The reason I remember this story so well is that over the course of the next several minutes, my own life changed; the way I viewed broken people (myself included) changed.

Sometimes we run on empty.

In a perfect world, all of our **resources** would have kept our life full.

I drew a bucket on a blank sheet of paper. "Sis, God intended your life to be like a bucket, full and running over with love, joy, and peace to pour on those He puts in your life. We live in a broken world though. There are really two problems we 'buckets' face. First, He places people in our lives to help fill us up, but sometimes those people fail. Second, sin causes holes in our bucket, and we leak."

I continued, "You need to know that not only are *you* hurt, but sin has hurt *everyone else* in your world. Because they are hurt, it may be they *couldn't* meet your needs, rather than they *wouldn't* meet your needs." I listened as she described how the "resource people" in her life had sins that crippled them. Very carefully, I helped her evaluate how these relationships had affected her life.

We then identified how her sin and the sin of those God intended to care for her had cut holes in her "bucket." No wonder she felt empty. It was a difficult process, and she wept. Eventually, as she dried her eyes, I said, "Sis, the Lord wants you to be filled with love and joy so you can pour your love out on everyone in your world. He wants to help you. Are you ready to begin this process of restoration and forgiveness?" She was.

I began to draw a cut on her bucket for each hurt. "Your parents abandoned you, and you felt so lost and unwanted. The unkind words spoken to you over the years pierced your heart. You decided that even God must not care about you. Those who molested you robbed you of your innocence and violated your fragile trust. The man who raped you wounded you deeply. You 'cut' yourself when you gave sex in the hopes you'd be loved, when you had the abortion, and then again when you tried to kill yourself."

The bucket I had drawn, now had many cuts. It was terribly damaged and leaked.

I asked, "Do you see your problem? First, your resources are damaged and haven't given much to you. Second, your bucket has holes in it, so you leak! No matter what goodness God pours into your bucket, or how often your husband or children say, 'I love you,' it's never enough. Even when you hear that God loves you, you leak, so those words of love and affirmation don't last very long and you always feel so empty."

I took her by the hand and asked her, "Are these scars from when you tried to take your own life?" She nodded. I slapped at her scarred wrists and asked, "Does that hurt?" "No," she replied. "Why not?" I asked. She said "Because it's healed!" I asked, "Sis, would you like the open wounds in your heart and memory to be healed just like that?" She replied, "Oh yes!" I explained that it is a process of restoration—a process of forgiveness and healing that is only possible through Christ.

Taking the Pain to Christ

I knew she worked in the medical field, and so I said, "If someone is in a car wreck and they come to you all cut up, what do you do?" She said, "We clean and disinfect the wounds and stitch them up." As she spoke, I began placing "stitches" across the cuts in her bucket. At that moment she exclaimed, "Bill, those look like little crosses!"

And sure enough, they did. "Sis, just like the cut on your wrist no longer hurts and all that is left is a scar, the Lord will cleanse and heal the hurts in your life so they are only memories, instead of open

wounds. Take your hurts to Him and ask Him to help you forgive those who have hurt you (see the next chapter for more on forgiving others), and confess your sins because He will forgive you . . . and then YOU can forgive yourself!" As Christians we can take our own sins to the Lord, receive forgiveness, and begin again.

♦ 1 John 1:9: *If we confess our sins, He is faithful and just to forgive us our sins and to cleanse us from all unrighteousness.*

It's almost like breathing. We breathe in oxygen, exhale, and breathe in another breath of fresh air.

Are You Damaged Goods?

As you look at your life, what damage has sin done in your life? Do you feel like damaged goods? You can't go back and "fix it," but because of Jesus Christ, you can start over.

There are times when the memories, the regrets, still come back to haunt me, and I find it impossible to ignore them. I then have to make a decision. I can hold onto them, trying not to remember my past failures and hurts or trying to convince myself to "feel" forgiven, or I can give them up to God. If I choose to dwell on each ugly chapter, I can feel the love, joy, and peace in my life drain out of me. I am learning to take my hurts and regrets to the Lord *again and again.* When I experience His forgiveness and claim His promises, I can forgive—even myself.

I'm still learning how to forgive myself.

PS: How's your bucket?

Dear Family and Friends,

Have things happened in your life that you just can't leave behind? Forget? Ignore? For me, those terrible memories are more like a snapshot than a moving picture. Snapshots stay frozen in time, but moving pictures move from one scene to the next.

In my life, one snapshot was held in the secret place of my mind. Because I kept it alive by remembering it, by feeding it my hate and fear, I couldn't—or wouldn't—go on in my life! Because I couldn't forgive someone else, or turn him over to God for judgment, I had a hard time feeling forgiven myself for the bad choices I had made in my own life. Sin freezes us in the past; God's grace lets us move into the future.

What was that snapshot? From the time I was a small child until I was nearly 40 years old, I kept an ugly secret from everyone. I had been molested.

I wish I had told my parents, but I didn't. I wish I had told my Grandpa or someone, but I didn't. I wish I had known how to turn the man over to the Lord for judgment, but I didn't. When you keep secrets, they are like an infection that can make you sick and even cause you to die.

I want to tell you how the Lord is helping me to learn to forgive myself and others—and how to start becoming a healthy person.

Thanks for reading.
Dad/Grandpa/Bill

CHAPTER FOUR

When You Don't Want to Forgive Others

From my Journal

The man who molested me 46 years ago walked into my room, and I felt ten years old all over again. I felt chills. I almost vomited.

Have hurts come into your life that you have had trouble forgiving?

Do those hurts in the past still hurt so much that you can't or won't forgive them?

I understand.

Were you abused as a child? Abandoned by a parent? Raped? Was your mate unfaithful? Was someone you loved murdered? Did someone introduce your child to drugs? Were you "laid off" after years of faithful service and then stripped of your retirement? Did a drunken driver cause an accident and take a loved one's life?

Do you understand with your head what you are supposed to do, but you can't, or refuse to, forgive them from your heart?

For me, *forgiving others isn't easy. It's not just difficult, because unless the Lord helps me, it's impossible!* I don't know how you are doing in your life, but for me, there is no area of my life where I need more help from the Lord than in the area of forgiving. I just can't do it by myself. I've tried! I've tried to ignore the pain, tried to forget the memories, tried to keep myself so busy that I can't think. Thousands of times I have said the words, "I can't forgive!" Another thousand times I've said, "I won't forgive them." I've listened to my culture and blamed my past and present problems on those who hurt me.

Since I've become a Christian, I've learned that I'm supposed to forgive. So, another thousand times I've said the words, "I forgive," only to take the forgiveness back in order to feed my bitterness or to use the pain as an excuse for my own sin. It's easier to preach or teach about forgiveness than to practice it.

I love the part of my Christian life where I get forgiven! When God forgives me, He totally cancels my debt. He "gives me what I need, not what I deserve!" He writes across the debt I owe Him, "Debt Cancelled!" He grants me, one who should be condemned, "a full pardon." When it comes to my sin, I want forgiveness from God, my mate, and children. When God adds up my sin, I want Him to add it up with Heaven's addition:

> ## Me + My Sin = Guilt
> ### but it can become
> ## Me + My Sin + Jesus = Forgiven!

The problem for me isn't wanting to receive God's forgiveness; my problem is being able to forgive those who have hurt me. In fact, sometimes I don't even want to WANT to forgive them! Even though I want God to give me what I need, not what I deserve, there are times I want God to give others what they deserve! Let me share with you how the Lord helped me with my struggle to forgive. I hope it brings you encouragement in your own personal struggle.

My Story

I was 56 years old. I was standing to teach a Bible lesson on forgiving others (God sure has a sense of humor), and in "**he**" walked. I couldn't believe that it was him! It was the man who molested me 46 years before, and I felt ten years old all over again. I felt chills and almost vomited. I began to shake, remembering how a once happy child became a boy with a crippled heart, who became a man with a crippled life.

I managed to finish the lesson, and I was grateful that he slipped away before I had to talk to him. I couldn't believe it; it was really him!

It was a long week. Forty-six years after he molested me, I was being confronted, not just with the molester and all the memories, but with ME! It was no longer what he could do to me, but what I would do with myself.

Let me share with you from my journal.

Lord, what do you want me to do? With my head I know that no matter what others have done to me, You want me to be whole and healthy. I know that I can only go forward if I'm able to forgive this man all over again . . . but Lord, the emotions I'm feeling, I'm not sure I could forgive him even if I wanted to. Lord, please help me get my feelings and memories back into Your hands and under Your control.

During the week, God was at work in my heart, and I reviewed what He says about being forgiven and being forgiving. We have all experienced hurtful situations. We are all called to forgive those who have hurt us. Sometimes we don't want to. When you have thoughts like these, remember what God's word says.

"Lord, what you teach about forgiveness is really hard to accept and harder to practice."

♦ Matthew 6:12,14-15 (NLT): *12And forgive us our sins, just as we have forgiven those who have sinned against us. 14If you forgive those who sin against you, your heavenly Father will forgive you. 15But if you refuse to forgive others, your Father will not forgive your sins.*

♦ Luke 6:27-38(NLT): Especially *38If you forgive others, you will be forgiven. If you give, you will receive. Your gift will return to you in full measure, pressed down, shaken together to make room for more, and running over. Whatever measure you use in giving — large or small — it will be used to measure what is given back to you.*

"Lord, it's easy to say the words 'I forgive,' but it's so hard to really mean them. I've said 'I forgive' him thousands of times, but unless You help me with my heart, I won't truly forgive him".

♦ Matthew 18:21-35 (NKJV): Especially *35So My heavenly Father also will do to you if each of you, from his heart, does not forgive his brother his trespasses.*

"Lord, I find myself being willing to say the words 'I forgive him only if . . .'"

- *If she says she's sorry first.*
- *If he asks me to forgive him.*
- *If he hasn't done this to others.*
- *If she has* truly *changed.*
- *If she promises to change her behavior.*
- *If he turns himself in to the police.*

- Then and only then *will I forgive.*

♦ Luke 17:3-5 (NLT): *I am warning you! If another believer sins, rebuke him; then if he repents, forgive him. Even if he wrongs you seven times a day and each time returns and asks forgiveness, forgive him.*

"Lord, unless you change my heart and give me the ability to forgive, I not only can't forgive him, I won't! Lord, that old hate for him returned again. Please help me! I don't want him as a brother, friend, or neighbor! I don't want to run into him at church!"

♦ 1 John 4:20: *If someone says "I love God" and hates his brother, he is a liar, for the one who does not love his brother whom he has seen, cannot love God whom he has not seen.*

What I Faced Was . . .

> # Me + My Sin + His Sin =
> # My Bitterness and Anger!

As I fought the battle inside of me to forgive, the Lord kept convicting me of my sin, His own righteousness, and His coming judgment of sinners (John 16:7-8). I wanted to give that man what he deserved rather than what he needed. But then I thought, "What if the Lord gave me what I deserved rather than what I needed?" I had said the words "I forgive him" thousands of times, and yet I couldn't forget what he'd done. . . . Then I remembered that forgiving does not remove the act from my memory.

Forgiving Is NOT Forgetting!

We never forget; we simply choose to turn them over to the Lord for His judgment of their sin, and we move forward again with our lives. I continued to think, "If I forgive him, he will get away with it!" But I knew that wasn't true. Forgiveness allows me to turn him over to God for punishment. It's no longer my responsibility to hate him or punish him. I needed to remember that he could fool me, but he can never fool God. God will know just how to judge him.

I thought, "But I don't FEEL like forgiving!" And then I remembered that forgiveness isn't a feeling. It's a decision, a choice. I argued, "I'm tired of this! How often do I have to forgive?" But I knew that I would have to *choose* to forgive *every time* I remembered for the rest of my life.

Finally I had to face the ramifications of forgiving him. I thought, "If I forgive, am I going to have to let him back into my life? Does forgiveness mean giving him a second chance to hurt me, my children, grandchildren, or my church?" Then I remembered that love and forgiveness are given unconditionally, but trust is earned. I remembered:

☞ I cannot include as my brother those God has not included, and I cannot exclude from my family those God has included.

☞ Forgiving the person who wronged me may or may not include letting him or her back into my life. I do not have to place that person in a position to hurt my family or church.

☞ There are sins that, unless repented of, God says eliminate people from Him and from His church.

> Note those God excludes (1 Cor 5:9-13; 1 Cor 6:9-10).
>
> Note those God includes (1 Cor 6:11).
>
> Note those I am to withdraw friendship or fellowship with (2 John 7-11).

Me + My Sin + His Sin + Jesus = My Ability to Forgive!

Back to My Story

From my journal: Morning, August 21

> I am fifty-six years old. The man who molested me when I was just ten years old attended Bible study last week. He had changed his name, but it was him. I knew if I ever saw him again, I would have to confront him, and so I've prayed, looked at God's Word, talked to Bobbi and my mentors, and prayed some more. I then shared my conclusions with the key leaders of the church. I knew that facing him would be difficult and I would need their love and support.

Evening, August 21

> He attended again tonight and I insisted that he meet with me privately. With my wife and the leaders watching from a distance, I walked up to him and said, "I need to see you in private." I then led him to the end of the hall. I had thought about it for 46

years. I'd prayed about it for 25 years. "What does the Lord want me to feel? What does God want me to say?"

Arriving at the end of the hall I said, "I have needed to talk to you ever since you molested me when I was a small boy. I need you to know how your selfish action affected my total life and how it took away my childhood." He looked shocked at my words. I said, "The morning after you molested me, I went downstairs in my uncle's home, and my parents and aunt and uncle were laughing. In my childish and confused emotional condition, I thought they knew what you had done and were laughing about it. In that moment, the Bill Putman that had existed died." I went on to tell him, "I'd been a happy kid before that. I had accepted the Lord and I'd wanted to be a minister. But in that one terrible experience, I no longer trusted God because He knew what you had done to me and didn't stop you. At that moment I thought my parents knew, so I couldn't trust them to protect me. I thought because you and my uncle were ministers, I could no longer trust the church."

I went on to explain to him that from that moment I stepped away from my faith and my family, and I began to wonder, "Am I a homosexual? What did that man see in my life that he would do that to me? God must not care about me."

I continued, "Your act upon my life started me down a path that nearly killed me." I went on to tell him how I started searching for who I am, and I fell into pornography, promiscuity, and deceit. I explained how I withdrew into myself and away from my family, failed in school, and how I finally came to the place of trying to kill myself. I paused, and he said nothing. I said, "What you did to me killed me . . . killed the person I was. I have grown to realize I can't blame you for the many bad decisions I made after that, but your act upon me set me up for failure and took away my innocence and childhood."

He said, "I don't remember doing that."

I quietly said, "That's a lie."

He said, "I didn't know what I did would have that effect upon you."

I said, "That too is a lie. You knew what you were doing was wrong and a sin, and in your selfishness, you chose to do it anyway." I said, "Have you molested others?" He said nothing. I took a deep breath and said, "I have been rescued by the Lord, but I wonder how many other children that you sinned against took their lives or will go to hell because of what you have done." Not looking me in the eye he said, "Will you forgive me?"

I said, "I forgave you many years ago and thousands of times since. In order to survive I turned you over to the Lord for judgment. I know that Satan used you. I don't hate you or want you to go to hell, but I do know that unless you gain forgiveness from the Lord, and unless you have repented and changed your behavior, you will go to hell." I said, "What is your present relationship to the Lord?"

He said, "I'm trying."

I said, "Are you still in the homosexual lifestyle?" He didn't answer, but just looked at the floor. I said, "Will you let me pray with you?"

He said, "Yes."

With great difficulty I put my hand on his shoulder and prayed, "Lord, thank you for being with me through all the pain of my childhood. Thank you for forgiving me for the terrible choices that I've made." I took a deep breath and said, "Father I don't want this man to go to hell. Would you please help him truly repent for his sins and let you forgive him and change him. Father, I would like him to be in heaven."

When I finished praying I said, "I have forgiven you, but as the minister of the church, I don't trust you. Unless you have truly repented, and are ready to change your behavior, I cannot have you attend this church again." He said nothing. I asked him to turn around and look down the hallway. I said, "Those men are the leaders of this church, and I have told them what you did to me and what I'm saying to you." He said nothing. I told him, if he truly wanted to be right with God, that I thought God would help me and the leaders of this church to help restore him. I concluded by saying he could attend this church only if he had truly repented and would accept help and counsel in being restored to God. He said nothing and left.

I returned to my wife and the leaders absolutely exhausted. Bobbi and God held onto me tightly that night.

From my journal two days later

Lord, thank You for helping me. In my flesh, one minute I wanted to run from that man and in the next minute I wanted to beat him to within an inch of his life. Thank You for lessening the hurt and hate and giving me pity for him. Lord, only You know the ways Satan used that man to hurt me and try to end my life and hopes. Lord, only You know the others he has hurt, but I thank You for being with me all those years and for helping me face the man who started me down an ugly path to self destruction. I love You Lord.

Seven years later

As I work on this chapter today, I'm amazed how seldom I'm haunted by the memories of what that man did to me. It still slips into my thoughts from my memory when I hear about another being molested, and I have to go to the Lord and ask for help in forgiving him all over again.

As a dad and pastor, I've concluded that if the man has true repentance and a tremendous change in his life, he can be forgiven, but I also believe that his choices in the past may eliminate or certainly severely restrict him from ever being around children. If he is fully restored to God, he could become a part of our spiritual family, but trust would have to be earned over time and he would always be watched, held accountable, and made to accept long-term counseling.

> **Him + Jesus + True Change + Time = Possible Restored Fellowship**

Pray for me. I *want* to be forgiving, but sometimes I just *want to want* to be forgiving.

Until I'm forgiven, I can't forgive. When I'm forgiven, I have God's help to forgive!

Truths to Hold On To

1. Only when we have God's forgiveness for our own sins and His help, can we forgive others. Forgiveness is not easy. It's not just difficult, without God it's downright impossible! I can't give away what I don't have. I can't truly forgive anyone until I'm truly forgiven.

2. Forgiveness is a choice. We are commanded to forgive, but it is a conscious act of our will, not something we usually *feel* like doing.

3. I need God's forgiveness every time I sin, and I need God's help in forgiving those who have sinned against me. Forgiveness must take place moment by moment, day by day.

4. Forgiveness doesn't mean forgetting. We often remember the hurt and at times feel the hurts. We must choose to forgive **every time** we remember, or we become a victim all over again.

5. Forgiveness is a lifelong process. The deeper the wound, the longer the denial, the more you hate the person who hurt you, the longer the process of forgiveness will take.

6. My forgiving them doesn't erase their consequences. Everyone affected by the sin will have consequences, memories, and fears to deal with. I can forgive and turn them over to God for judgment but everyone hurt will have to live with the consequences the sin brings.

Dear Friends and Family,

I can tell you the day that I finally remembered again that being a Christian is not me working on me, but Jesus living and working in me. It was December 11, 1971. The Lord gave me back my hope, and on that night I wrote:

He's Still Working on Me

The great God of heaven, began to paint one day
And with a brush and canvas, with paints from red to gray,
With strokes as bold as thunder, as lightning it did glow,
It was the life of a child, and it started white as snow.
The picture looked majestic in the image of God's Son,
And the artist smiled with pleasure for soon He'd have it done.
But the picture was not finished when tragedy struck one day,
For from the hands of the Master, the brush was snatched away.
Yes, God, He had been painting on a canvas not yet done,
A picture filled with joy and peace in the image of His Son,
But when I sinned I took away the brush from God's own hand,
And tried to paint my own picture, but friend, please understand,
The picture turned from beauty, to pain and cold despair,
I painted then with guilt and hate until only black was there.
But then one day I came to know that with mighty strokes of red,
My God could take my strokes away, and place His there instead.
Now once again, He has the brush, and although He's still not done,
My life's becoming now conformed to the Image of His Son.

Bill Putman, December 11, 1971

I know if you take a good look at my picture, you will see many unfinished places. But please be patient: when Jesus, the artist, finishes with me, I'm going to be something wonderful. Who's painting your picture?

Love,
Dad/Grandpa/Friend

CHAPTER FIVE

When Life Seems Hopeless

From my journal: December of 1971

I've lost all hope. I've tried to fix myself, my mate, my children and my friends. It's just not working . . . what do I do now?

I was ready to leave my marriage, family, and ministry. The week I was planning on "resigning," a friend encouraged me to try again, and this time to let the Lord fix my broken heart and broken family.

How Did We Become Broken?

I want to assure you that I never got up one morning and thought to myself, "I think I'll be a lousy dad and husband today," but so often I was. Sometimes I had my eyes on the problems within me, or the ones surrounding me, and I fell into deep depression. Sometimes I had my eyes on my own battles, and I forgot the battles my loved ones were fighting. Sometimes Bobbi and I were struggling in marriage, and we didn't have any answers for ourselves or anyone else. Sometimes we were struggling with our jobs, finances, or health. Sometimes it was the rebellion of one (or more) of the kids that sunk us into a crushing despair. For all our efforts, we were a mess.

When My Plans Failed, I Started Looking for "Plan B"

As I look back, what our broken family needed was a change in ownership and management. The physical dad and mom in our family needed their heavenly Father to come into their broken lives and rebuild their hearts. We needed Him to make our house into a home so that when our prodigal children quit running, there would be a real home for them to come home to!

Down through my life, I've looked at other people's lives, homes, or ministries and thought, "Look at them, they have all the right training and gifts, but no one is following them!" In the middle of our "broken family period," I took a look in the mirror at myself. I saw one of those "husbands," "dads," and "leaders" looking back at me. I had all the right qualifications for being a husband, dad, and a minister, and yet when all the individual parts of my life were packaged into me, I failed to have the one qualification for leadership:

No one was following me!

I was giving my family good orders. I was reading good books. As a minister I was preaching good sermons (unless you didn't like the people I was "borrowing" them from). I had good plans that worked for other successful people, parents, or ministers. But my home and church seemed, to me, to be just buildings full of empty people. I came to realize that the people in my life were listening to my words but they were not following my steps. Even worse than that, my own children were not following me.

In my harassed and helpless condition I started looking for someone else to blame. I thought, "It must be my family's fault—or the church's! I'll change them." In my desperate search, I decided that if I could just find the right book or the right counselor then I would know how to be a better husband, dad, and friend. I reasoned, "If I could only get my prodigal children to a counselor, we could be a happy family!" I lamented, "If I had only been older when we had children" and "If only my wife were able to stay home with the children instead of working outside of the home, we wouldn't be in this mess!" I tortured myself, "If only I could afford to keep the children in Christian school!" If only . . . If only . . . If only. . . . The "if only's" were killing me!

I needed to start changing the only one
I could make decisions for . . . me!

Until my own life was turned over to the Lord so He could begin making my mess into a miracle, no book, church or counselor, no class, no two-parent home or Christian school could bring about the changes necessary to have my family not only listen to my words, but follow my life.

> **M**y family didn't need a critic or a conscience. They didn't need me to be a better parent; they needed me to become transPARENT so they could see the Lord at work in my life!
>
> **T**hey needed the hope that would come from knowing, "If God can change my dad, he can change me too!"

I finally came to understand that I needed God to take me, a broken down poor excuse for a husband, dad, and minister, and allow Him to change my life—to make me into a miracle. After all, I knew in my head that parents who can't even read or do not know any counselors, can raise godly, well-adjusted children. Families with young parents often raise great kids. Single-parent homes, broken from divorce, have produced Christian kids. Parents who raise their children in public schools can still raise wonderful godly children. Even families where neither of the parents are a Christian often produce godly children!

I remember my brother-in-law saying, "There's nothing wrong with your children that getting yourself under control wouldn't help." Ouch! But it was true; I needed to start working on the only one I could really make decisions for, instead of trying to change everyone else in my world. I needed to let the Lord be the head of our home and my wife and me *partner* in raising our children. It was after that decision to surrender my life that, in spite of the crisis in my home, people started really listening to my sermons and following my example. They didn't follow me because I was right. They followed me because they could see God at work in my life!

How Are Things at Your House?

Have your plans failed? Have you exhausted yourself by trying to find solutions? Are you convinced anything short of a miracle won't be enough?

I needed a miracle and nothing less!

I don't know how it is in your life, but sometimes I'm not experiencing joy or satisfaction in my Christian walk. There are other times, though, when my heart is ready, and the Scriptures transform my mind and life.

I remember reading Luke 4:18-21. Jesus entered the temple, picked up the Scriptures, and read from Isaiah. In Luke 4:20 it says, "*He (Jesus) closed the book and gave it back to the attendant, and sat down; and the eyes of all in the synagogue were fixed upon Him. And he began to say to them, 'Today this scripture has been fulfilled in your hearing.'*"

I was intrigued and wanted to know more about what He said that was being fulfilled, so I looked at Isaiah 61. Here is the full text of what Jesus was saying:

> ¹The Spirit of the Sovereign LORD is on me, because the LORD has anointed me to preach good news to the poor. He has sent me to bind up the brokenhearted, to proclaim freedom for the captives and release from darkness for the prisoners, ²to proclaim the year of the LORD's favor and the day of vengeance of our God, to comfort all who mourn ³and provide for those who grieve in Zion — to bestow on them a crown of beauty instead of ashes, the oil of gladness instead of mourning, and a garment of praise instead of a spirit of despair. They will be called oaks of righteousness, a planting of the LORD for the display of his splendor. ⁴They will rebuild the ancient ruins and restore the places long devastated; they will renew the ruined cities that have been devastated for generations. . . . ⁶And you will be called priests of the LORD, you will be named ministers of our God!

When I read the above passage I suddenly realized that He was not only making this statement to the people then, but to me and my family now! Think of it. . . . Jesus said to those people, "This scripture has been fulfilled in your hearing!" As I read those promises, I asked the Lord to make me a miracle, and as He began to change me, it gave me growing confidence that He could change my marriage, my family, and my world.

As He began to change me, I discovered that *He can* bring good news!

- *He can* bind up the brokenhearted!
- *He can* set the captive free (He's setting my filthy life and mind free!)
- *He can* make this a favorable year!
- *He can* bring comfort to my grieving heart!
- *He can* fill my heart with joy and my mouth with praise!
- *He can* rebuild the ruins of my life!

There is encouragement in what He did in the past, but there is outrageous joy and confidence in knowing He's still keeping His word and making a miracle out of me! **He can, He could, He would, and He did!** I can become joy-filled and contented! I can be married to a joy-filled, secure wife! We can see God reach out to reclaim each member of our family, ***one person at a time!***

Dear Family and Friends,

When I first met Bobbi my life was confusing to me. I felt as if I didn't have even one true friend, and it seemed that every time I tried anything, I failed. I was having a hard time believing in God and trying to forgive myself. I was trying to make up for all my failures by working for God.

I've never understood what she saw in me, but she loved me and believed in me—even when I didn't believe in myself.

Did you know that:

— Our first date was miniature golf?
— I asked her to marry me in the Bible college prayer room?
— After asking her to marry me, I tried to get out of the whole marriage thing, so we were engaged seven times in six months?
— We were married on the Fourth of July at 2:00 pm, left the church at 4:00, and our car blew up at 6:30? (I called a friend, and his dad came to our rescue. He towed our car to their home. We went with them to the fireworks, and our first meal together was cold pizza!)
— Our first home was a 23-foot-long trailer house?

We sure had a lot of adventures together, but I want you to know the most important way God has used her in my life. I watched God make a miracle out of her. I decided that if He could make a difference in her, maybe He can make a difference in me!

I hope as you read this that you will discover if God can make a miracle out of us, He can do the same thing for you!

Thanks for reading.
Dad/Grandpa Bill

CHAPTER SIX
When You Feel Inadequate

When You See God Make Someone You Know into a Miracle, It Gives You Hope!

I once read of a man in the Second World War who, when in the middle of a battlefield, with bombs and bullets flying all around him, was forced out of his safe position. He got up, ran across the field and jumped into a large hole. When he caught his breath, he noticed he wasn't alone in the hole, there was a man standing there holding a crucifix and screaming, "How do you make this thing work?"

If you are trusting in a cross, a church, a Bible, a parent, or a person, your trust is misplaced. Maybe you've tried to live up to what you think a Christian is, but, because you don't have Christ, you have tried to live your life in your own strength, and you feel empty and incomplete. Authentic Christianity is having a relationship with God and having Him live in and through you.

Consider the little girl who walked with her grandfather every morning in hopes of seeing his prize roses in bloom. After several disappointing mornings, the grandpa was awakened from his nap to the sound of his little granddaughter crying. He looked down to see her tear-filled eyes. In her hand she held one of his prize roses all torn apart. She looked up and said, "Grandpa, I couldn't wait so I tried to blossom it myself."

Those who know me best know that there have been times when I've tried to blossom my own life, marriage, or family. I've had to stand before God like that little girl, with my heart, marriage, and home broken. I'm glad our story doesn't have to end with our failure because God wants to work in our lives!

A Love Story

I love the fact that God started working in our original parents at CREATION.

God says in Genesis 1:26-27 that we are created "in His image." We were intended to rule, to dominate, to be fruitful, and to multiply. God created us to be like Him, to be loved by Him, and to love Him in return. He created us to worship Him here and spend eternity with Him.

I love that God started working on us as individuals at PRO-CREATION.

Psalm 139:13-16 teaches us that God started working on us at conception, when the sperm hit the egg. While we were in the womb, God had already started making us into His image.

I hate the tragedy of human history when each of us sinned.

We turned from God and tried to do things our own way (Rom 3:10,23). When each of us sinned, it destroyed God's original intention for us which was to make us into the image of God. Ephesians 2:1,8,12 tells us that we became spiritually dead, living like the world, ruled by Satan, disobedient, separated from Christ, excluded, strangers, without hope, without God.

I love it when the love of God invaded our world through RE-CREATION.

Jesus came, not to restore what we had lost, but us! Ephesians 2:4-5 says, "But God, is so rich in mercy, and he loved us so very much, that even while we were dead because of our sins, he gave us life when He raised Jesus from the dead." When Jesus becomes our Savior and the Holy Spirit moves into our hearts, we become a *re-creation*!

♦ Ephesians 2:1-3 tells me what I was without Jesus: *¹Once you were dead, doomed forever because of your many sins. ²You used to live just like the rest of the world, full of sin, obeying Satan, the mighty prince of the power of the air. He is the spirit at work in the hearts of those who refuse to obey God. ³All of us used to live that way, following the passions and desires of our evil nature. We were born with an evil nature, and we were under God's anger just like everyone else.*

♦ Ephesians 2:4 tells me how Christ saved me, "But God . . . .": *⁴But God is so rich in mercy, and he loved us so very much . . .*

♦ Ephesians 2:8-10 tells me how He is making my life brand new! *⁸God saved you by his special favor when you believed. And you can't take credit for this; it is a gift from God. ⁹Salvation is not a reward for the good things we have done, so*

none of us can boast about it. [10]For we are God's masterpiece. He has created us anew
in Christ Jesus, so that we can do the good things he planned for us long ago.

We begin to see Him working through everything in our lives to make us a prepared person for a prepared place! He begins to blossom us!

> *When you become a Christian,*
> *you begin to become a miracle!*
> *When others see the changes God makes,*
> *it gives them hope that they too can change!*

My Story

I've had the joy of watching a "blossoming miracle" for 42 years. Let me explain where great people come from. The following are excerpts from a letter I wrote to my children.

A letter to my children:

I bet you think your mom must be superwoman, not just a super woman, but *Superwoman!* Where did this miracle come from?

- ✗ She was a little girl from a fatherless home whose mother was tormented by fears and doubts.
- ✗ Her teenage years were filled with loneliness, and she never wanted to go back to a high school reunion because of all those lonely memories.
- ✗ She was a girl who thought she was ugly because of her complexion or a thousand other reasons.
- ✗ She married a difficult man and has stayed married for forty plus years.
- ✗ She gave birth to five children in six and one half years who grew up to be five teenagers all at once.
- ✗ She had her mother live with her the last years of her life.
- ✗ She has been the wife of an often-depressed man and she is your loyal friend.
- ✗ She has been a church planter's wife (who often moved), a minister's wife, and the Director of Recruitment for a Bible college.
- ✗ At this moment she is working full-time as a Bible college ministry leader at Real Life Ministry, continuing her education, and a Red Cross volunteer.

I'll bet you've asked, "How did she do it?" "How did she keep up?" or thought, "I must not be made of the same stuff she is."

You don't remember the hard days.

When we were newly married, it seemed to me that she was afraid of everything. She would stand in the driveway crying when I went out of town because she was afraid something would happen to me, or that something would come up and she wouldn't know how to handle it. She was afraid to have people over to the house unless I was there because she thought "I don't have anything to say," and "They aren't here to see me anyway."

There were difficult years when she had so many babies to care for or when her health was broken and her emotions were on the very edge. You don't remember when the church stepped in to provide meals and housecleaning. You may not remember when she was very close to emotional exhaustion. You don't remember when the doctor told me that she had leukemia and we might lose her (Jim was nine, Melissa eight, Joni six, Angela five, and Melody was just three). Those were difficult times. Our marriage was stressed and our finances were strained.

We certainly have had our share of troubles, but somehow we made it one day at a time, one bill at a time, one problem at a time, one health crisis at a time, one job change at a time. We persevered through babies and diapers, chicken pox and mumps. There were lonely days when she sacrificed her own education to get us all through school, and she waited while I ministered to others. She put her needs aside to help with my problems and needs. She went through times without friends (or no time to spend with friends), through children not finding friends (or finding the wrong friends), through the heartaches of no adults to talk to because of babies to care for, and through your difficult teen years when you sometimes thought only of yourselves. She worked hard to provide clothes for a growing family and persevered through the rebellion of children (and all of us living with the consequences of their choices). She suffered through the death of her first grandchild and through the silence and withdrawal of a daughter because of an abuse she knew nothing about. She sat on the bed with you many nights trying to answer the unanswerable and trying to help you see that the most important thing you can offer people is friendship. She struggled through conflicts—when she stood as a buffer between you and my anger and frustration. There were so many times she focused on her family's needs and tried to shield us from noticing her many needs that went unmet.

What a Woman! How Did She Do It?

What do you see in Mom now? Superwoman? Super wife? Super Mom? Super friend? Super minister's wife? Super worker? I think God sees her just as she is, His faithful little girl, Bobbi, who He has been blossoming into the image of His Son Jesus.

How Did She Turn the Words of the Bible into Trust?

My most constant memory of your mom is that, no matter what time I'd get up, she was already up. Not to watch TV or clean the house, not to prepare the clothes or cook breakfast, not to have a few moments for her self. She was up early to spend time with her heavenly Father, to cry out to Him in her need, to write (journal) to Him of her concerns. Whether in the middle of a crisis or a time of peace, she ran to Him who promised that He would make all things work out for good, to look to her source of strength for the coming day, to talk to Him about you and me, and to just spend time with her most constant companion, her heavenly Father.

Over the years of spending time with her heavenly Father I've watched a girl become a woman because she allowed God to meet her needs. I watched God give her hope and strength, to pull her together when she was falling apart. She trusted God to help her weak husband to become a man of faith. She trusted God to help her with too many bills and too little income. She trusted God to work on her unfinished children who were often selfish and rebellious, often ignorant of her own needs to be appreciated and loved, whose children most often didn't even notice the things she did for them. She could get through because she believed her God was right there working, and He would keep His word to her.

It's Not That Your Mom Is a Great Woman . . . It's That She Has a Great God!

Well kids, I hope this letter doesn't make you feel like you don't measure up, or like you don't have the right stuff to follow in her steps. When Jesus becomes your Savior, He wants to blossom you into a miracle.

"Who can find a virtuous and capable wife?" I didn't find her; God grew her up right before my eyes. She has become a miracle, and I'm watching our family become a miracle, one day at a time. It wasn't that she tried hard and made it happen; she let go and let God!

A Project to Help You Understand How You Can Become "A Miracle in the Making"

♦ Romans 8:28-29 (NASB): *[28]And we know that God causes all things to work together for good to those who love God, to those who are called according to his purpose. [29]For those whom he foreknew, he also predestined to become conformed to the image of his Son, so that he would be the firstborn among many brethren.*

Problems We Will Face	God's Promises That Give Me Confidence

Romans 8:26–weakness
Romans 8:33–accusations
Romans 8:35-37–tribulation
    distress, persecution
    famine, nakedness,
    peril, sword,
    death, life, angels
    principalities,
    present trouble,
    future troubles,
    powers,
    heights,
    depth,
    created things
	Romans 8:36–Help from the Holy Spirit. He intercedes with the Father on my behalf.
	Romans 8:28–God causes all things to work together for good for those who love the Lord.
	Romans 8:29–God causes us to be conformed to the image of Jesus Christ. He calls, justifies, and glorifies.
	Romans 8:35–We are never separated from God's love.
	Romans 8:37–We will overwhelmingly overcome.

2 Corinthians 1:9: "That I might not trust myself but the God who raises the dead."

1. Please take a moment and list the weaknesses, trials, and difficulties that you are facing.

2. Reread Romans 8:26-37 and identify how the Lord has been working in your life to increase your faith.

3. Read 2 Corinthians 1:8-9 and identify the lesson Paul learned from his sufferings.

Dear Family and Friends,

I'm not very lucky. If it can break, it will. If I buy a house, I lose money on it. If I invest money in the stock market, I'll lose at least half. If I buy a lottery ticket, I don't even get one number right. If I try to fix it, I'll make it worse. I think some of my children believe they've inherited the "Putman Curse" because the same thing is happening to them.

I may not be very lucky, but I am something better; I'm blessed! Those who have watched my troubles have seen God come through anyway.

We have a God who loves us. We have children and grandchildren who love God and us. Our siblings are not only siblings, but true friends. We have true friends all over the world. We live in a wonderful house and work in a great church. Even though we have had limited resources or talents, God has used us to make a difference in people's lives. Who needs luck?!

We were not able to raise you in fancy houses with lots of expensive toys or even help much with college, but God has blessed you greatly! The Lord has given you mates and children who really love you, and together, you are accomplishing more in your lives, marriages, and children than we even dreamed.

I hope you will get a blessing out of reading what we've learned about trouble and the difference between "luck" and the "help and blessings" of God.

Thanks for reading.
Dad/Granddad/Bill

CHAPTER SEVEN

When Troubles Overwhelm You

"Into Every Life a Little Rain Must Fall . . . But This Is Ridiculous!"

One day I was so burdened with my own problems and the constant needs of people all around me that I felt completely drained—empty. I was working in the church office when I heard a car door slam, and I rushed to the window to see who it was. "Oh, no!" I thought. "I can't handle one more person!" I thought of hiding in the bathroom, but I noticed she was moving fast. I knew I didn't have time, so being the great man of God that I am, I hid under the desk!

After she left, I did what I should have done first. I took myself to God in prayer and asked Him to take my heavy load. I picked up the phone and called my dear friend and made an appointment to see her.

Maybe you can relate to my story. So, how are you doing? Tired is all right. Weary, overloaded, exhausted, and full of doubt and fear isn't.

I See the Heavy Load That Some of My Friends Are Carrying.

Some of my friends are weary because their children or grandchildren come home, not just for a visit, but to stay. Some of them are trying to carry the burden of a broken heart because of the unfaithfulness of their mate or of a divorce. Some of them have children who are in prison, are trapped in drugs or alcohol, or have made other destructive choices. Some of our friends are weary, overloaded, and overwhelmed because their loved one has Alzheimer's, diabetes, or a hundred other health issues that require their constant care. Others are enduring the exhaustion of a depression that just won't seem to go away. Some are filled with the cancer of worry that stands like a cloud over every second of their day. Some of my friends are disappointed and bitter at life and God and just can't try anymore. Some of my friends have taken their eyes off of Jesus and have lost their faith.

One day several years ago, while reading *Evidence That Demands a Verdict* (by Josh McDowell) I found the following letters.

GODISNOWHERE

Since then I have carried around cards with those letters on them with a small question printed underneath. . . . "Which do you see?" Take a close look. . . . Is it "God is **NO**where?" or "God is **NOW** here?" Both of these statements are made up of the same letters, but how you arrange the letters is critical to how you'll get through hard times.

God is NOwhere.

When I see "God is nowhere," I picture myself as an ox pulling a wagon with a heavy load through the mud. The ox pulls and tries until, stuck in the mud, it is too exhausted to go further. Sometimes in our weariness we conclude that God is nowhere! Our burdens weigh us down and we come grinding to a halt. When "God is NOwhere" in my heart, I can't help anyone else. When they come to me with their problems I want to yell, "Will you shut up? I don't want to know about your problems! *I want help with mine!*"

In those difficult times just "believing" isn't enough! Believing helps me know that Jesus came to "seek and to save sinners" (Luke 19:10 and John 20:30-31). It helps me know that when Jesus sees people in need He helps (Matt 9:36), and He feels compassion for them—like sheep without a shepherd. Believing helps me know that "God so loved the world that He gave His only begotten Son, that whosoever believes in Him should not perish but have eternal life" (John 3:16). But sometimes "believing" isn't personal; sometimes it's just a list of facts.

Knowing the historical evidence for the Bible and learning *about* Jesus supports my belief. It helps to have evidence that He was God in the flesh, evidence of His sinless life, and evidence of His miracles. It helps me believe His message—that He died on the cross to pay the price for the sins of all men and rose again to offer new life. The evidence helps me know, which helps me believe. But I need more than "belief."

When my head says, "God is now here," but my feelings say, "God is nowhere," I don't need more faith; I need trust! I need Jesus to step out of the Bible, the pictures, and sermons and be real to me! It has to be personal . . . so I can trust. Unless my belief turns to trust, I'm in trouble!

Are you there, God?

Consider John the Baptist, in jail, already sentenced to die. In Matthew 11:1-4 he reflects on his life, a life dedicated to God—to holy living and the ministry of proclaiming the savior, Jesus, to the world! But there he sat in prison, facing death. I love his honest words, "When John heard in prison what Christ was doing, he sent his disciples to ask him, 'Are you the one who was to come, or should we expect someone else?'" John was asking, "Is *God nowhere*, or is *God now here*?"

Imagine, John the Baptist had given his whole life to proclaiming the truth, but suddenly he was asking, "Was I right? Are You really the one? Did I waste my life? Is what I've spent my life living for, worth dying for?"

I love what Jesus did for John. When I'm burdened, I need Him to do the same thing for me. Jesus first sent some other believers to encourage John. Listen to the message He sent: *"Jesus answered and said to them, 'Go and report to John what you hear and see; the blind receive sight and the lame walk, the lepers are cleansed and the deaf hear, the dead are raised up, and the poor have the gospel preached to them'"* (Matt 11:4-5, NASB). He is essentially saying, "Yes, I'm the one, John. I'm still doing miracles! You are still my man!"

When I am tired, the Lord uses other believers, the Bible, a song, or a precious memory to remind me that no matter what I *feel* . . . **God is now here**. I might not be able to see what He is doing in *my* life, but He is working.

I have to admit that sometimes I don't want to hear the encouragement He sends, and I'd rather have a pity party. Sometimes I am so tired, burdened, and self-absorbed, that when I hear of *others'* blessings, or see *others* getting their prayers answered, it only adds to my heavy load.

God is NOW here . . . COME!

I'm so glad that in Matthew 11 Jesus gives further instructions for His weary followers.

♦ Matthew 11:28-30: [28]*Come unto me, all you who are weary and burdened, and I will give you rest.* [29]*Take my yoke upon you and learn from me, for I am gentle and humble in heart; and you will find rest for your souls.* [30]*For My yoke is easy and My burden is light.*

Looking closer, Jesus says:

1. **"Come."** Jesus always invites. He never forces.

2. "Come unto **Me**." It's personal. I am to come to a person, *The* person, Jesus. Too often I find myself looking to a book, a seminar, a worship service, a significant Christian leader, or a counselor when only Jesus can satisfy my needs. "Come unto *Me!*"

3. "Come unto me **all** *who are heavy burdened*." The only requirement for coming to Him is being tired and overburdened. He excludes none. I don't have to feel, act, or do "right" to be qualified to "Come to Him."

4. "Come to me . . . **Take My yoke upon you**." We see that Jesus is asking, "Give Me your burden; you cannot carry it by yourself. Exchange your single yoke and team up with Me. Take My double yoke, and we'll carry it together!"

My Single Yoke
I Can't Carry
by Myself

The Double Yoke
Jesus Carries
with Me

5. "Come . . . Take My yoke upon you and **learn from me**." I believe that He is inviting us to team up with Him. We begin the Christian walk with Jesus walking beside us to teach us how to live our lives. He promises that even when we are weak or we stumble like little children, He will be gentle with us.

6. "Come . . . You will find **rest for your souls**." In this passage Jesus talks of two different "rests," one He gives (11:28) and the other He helps us find (11:29). The first rest comes when our sins are forgiven. The second rest He helps us find as we walk beside Him, as He helps with the everyday circumstances of our lives.

During the first year I was restored to the Lord I found this comforting poem:

He Went That Way Before

"The road is rough," I said. "My Lord,
There are stones that hurt me so."
And He said, "Dear child, I understand,
I walked it long ago."
"My burden," I said, "Is far too great;
How can I bear it so?"
"My child," said He, "I know its weight;
I carried my cross, you know."
"But," I said, "If there were friends
Who would make my way their own . . ."
"Ah yes!" He said, "Gethsemane
Was hard to face alone."
And so I climbed the stony path
Content at last to know,
That where my Master had not gone,
I would not need to go.
And strangely then, I found new friends.
The burdens grew less sore,
As I remembered, long ago,
He went that way before.
—Leone Bays

From Belief to Trust

We can't trust Him unless we know Him personally. How long has it been since you've taken time to *listen* to God? The Lord has given us His Word, His Christians, His Church, and His Communion to remind us who He is and what He promises.

How long has it been since you *honestly talked* to God in prayer? When I struggle with my prayer life, I sit down at my computer and just vent my feelings to the Lord. I pour out all my feelings—get it all out! I can't fool Him, so why hold back what I am feeling? When I'm finished, I delete the parts I don't mean and then I read it to my Heavenly Father.

Here is a prayer from my journal during a difficult time:

Lord, I'm overwhelmed today. Yesterday I was flooded with wounded people whose troubles were so far beyond my ability to help, let alone understand. Over the day I noticed I started being more and more tired and stressed, and I think that I was trying to help these people in my own strength.

Lord, today, right now, before the next person calls or comes in, please help me remember that I don't have a single yoke I have to carry all by myself. Help me remember that you said, 'Come unto Me,' and You will share the load of those who come to me.

Lord, I love you. Thanks for reminding me I can't face life on my own; I never could. I've always needed You!

Bill.

Today I read this chapter to a man who is in the last stages of cancer. Unless the Lord chooses to add to his life, he will soon be in heaven. As I read this to him, I asked him what he does when nothing he's tried seems to work. He said, "Unless the Lord shows up, I'm sunk. But I believe God is always there, whether I feel like He is or not."

Sometimes I trust. Sometimes I want to trust. Often I just want to **want** to trust, and God is faithful anyway!

Family and Friends,

Depression.

How come I never see it coming?

How come my answers for depression always sound so good when I'm giving advice to others but don't work for me?

I remember one Christmas when all my children had come home—but one. The family was upstairs having such a great time sharing about what was going on in their lives and getting ready for our Christmas celebration, but I was down in the basement suffering from depression. Melissa left the family fun upstairs and came downstairs to try to help me. She said, "Daddy, can't you just be happy that the rest of us are home?" She was right. I wanted to. I should have been able to, but frankly, I just couldn't.

Depression. I hate it. It makes strong people weak, intelligent people into fools, decisive people incapable of reason, and the sensitive into blubbering idiots.

As you read this chapter on depression, I hope you do what I'm learning to do rather than what I did.

Sometimes nothing and no one can help but Jesus!

Thanks for reading,
Dad/Grandpa Bill

CHAPTER EIGHT

When You Are Depressed and Don't Know Why

From my journal during a time in the pit of depression:

Lord, I've been coming to you, crying out in pain for months. Please help me, Lord. I need Your help to get my eyes up, to follow the counsel I give to others . . . to just shut up about "How I feel" and "What I want." Lord, I've been beating myself up with every breath. In a year when our family has never been better, Satan, the "accuser of the brethren" is tempting me to forget the good You have done through my life and drawing my focus to only the broken parts and the efforts that didn't work out as I hoped.

Please help me to get control of my feelings and my mouth. I'm getting in the way of Your using my life. I've been to the doctor to see if something is <u>physically</u> wrong and I'm asking You for a good report. If something physical is wrong though, please help the doctor to find it and help me. If I am falling apart <u>emotionally</u>, please help me find a counselor to help . . . and then help me listen to his advice and counsel. If I need to take medicine, please humble me, and help me to take the advice I give others.

Lord, I know I'm <u>spiritually</u> empty. I know I've been working for You and not allowing You to work in and through me. I've been hiding from my depression, and so I've been pushing and stressing. I've been trying to be a 40-watt bulb in a 150-watt-bulb area. I know I've been <u>focusing on the negative</u> rather than the positive, and I've become critical of myself and others.

Lord, I know You love me, but I'm having trouble loving me. Why can I accept that You love and forgive me, but I can't give love and forgiveness to myself? I'm giving others the right answers, but I'm not accepting them myself. I'm believing in You, Lord, but I'm not trusting.

Please help my emotions and mouth to be yielded to Your control.

I love You.

Bill

I'm not sure if everyone gets depressed. Some people either are never depressed or they lie. I've fought the battle of depression all my life, and because my dad and brothers have also fought this battle, our family calls it "The Putman Pout."

How Come I Never See It Coming?

Have you noticed that depression sneaks up on you—that you seldom see it coming until it happens? I know that our "buckets" leak and we get empty. But why do we "stay there"—especially when we've been there before? Instead of focusing on the Lord, and the wonderful things He has done and is doing in our lives, all we can see are the broken pieces, and we fall into the pit of depression.

I've noticed that when people get empty, their natural human tendencies are exaggerated. Some quiet people become silent. Some people, who struggle with anger, lose control. People with weight struggles eat. Some with moral or ethical weaknesses compromise and indulge. Some open and talkative people become really hard to be around. When depression descends on me, the normal discouragements of life overwhelm me, and I become obsessed with finding solutions and "fixing" things.

Have you noticed that when we get "empty," we lose control? We don't seem to be able to stop ourselves before driving ourselves (and those we love most) crazy. Maybe it's because we *slide* into the depression rather than fall into it. Instead of taking time to rest, pray, and reflect, I worked harder at trying to fix my problems. Instead of stepping back, I pushed harder. Instead of letting God lead, empower, and work through me, I pressed on and became overwhelmed with **my** emotions, **my** work, **my** talking, and **my** self-value (or lack of).

Since I have been a Christian, there have been at least six times when my "bucket" became empty. Looking back I can identify when my **physical** bucket, **marriage** bucket, **parenting** bucket, **health** bucket, **job** bucket, and **dream** bucket each became empty. These were all different areas of my life, but the results were the same!

Why Does This Keep Happening?

Maybe there's really just one bucket, a **spiritual** bucket, that has different areas of vulnerability. In each of the above situations, it's as if my bucket sprung a small leak or two in one area, and before I knew it, there was a great hemorrhage!

Looking back, I can clearly recall the Lord showing me my broken self in each situation. I saw the leaks, but I didn't like what I saw. In each case, I had embarrassed myself in front of people I really admired, or whose approval really meant something to me. I had "failed."

A journal entry after one such time:

> Lord, it's happened again. I didn't see it coming, but here I sit in my pit of depression. In this latest situation, I was tired and drained, and I wasn't in control of my emotions or words. It's hard to look at myself through the eyes of those I love most and see what they must see—a man silent, afraid to speak, or a man who just won't shut up! Surely I was a man out of control, self-absorbed, tired, and "bleeding" on anyone who would listen.

Can you identify the major times in your life when you became empty, and depression raised its ugly head?

Why Do We Get Depressed?

I counsel people nearly every day, and I suppose there are a whole lot of reasons people get depressed. I have found it helpful to work through a sort of inventory to identify the main cause.

? Is Jesus really *your* Savior?

Some people are depressed because they are trying to be a Christian without having Christ! In that case, they are reading the Bible looking for answers, but it's as if they are reading someone else's mail. The Bible is a love letter to Christians, those God has forgiven and empowered to produce the Christian life. We can have Christian parents, be raised in a Christian home (even one where the dad is a pastor), attend a growing church, know and usually obey all the "Christian rules," and still not know Jesus Christ as our Savior. In fact, I think that many "church kids," or people who are related to Christians, give "Christianity" a try only to discover they "can't make it work," and they give up. Remember, *you can't be a Christian without Christ!*

❓ Is Jesus *really* your Lord?

Sometimes depression comes because we Christians are trying to do God's job for Him. We accept the salvation, but we still want to be in charge! We want to do our own thing, or if we're going to do as God asks, we're going to do it in our own ability.

Let me illustrate. If you pick up your Bible and start reading in the middle of the Book of Ephesians (Eph 4:25–6:9) you will find 39 specific commands for every Christian. If you take the time to read them you will hear *"Don't!" "Do!" "Get rid of!" "Be!" "Forgive!" "Don't!" "Don't!"* . . . *"Don't!"* It's a tough assignment! I don't know about you, but I have a lot of problems living up to the commands of Scripture *with* Jesus as my Savior and Lord. Before He was my Savior I couldn't do them at all! *You can't live the Christian life without letting Jesus be Lord of your life!*

❓ How is your health?

Sometimes our depression is caused by something physical. How are you sleeping and eating? Are you getting enough exercise? Taking time off to rest? The depression may be caused by a change in your blood pressure or sugar levels. It may be a warning sign from God that something more serious is happening in your body. I believe "Doctor Luke" traveled with the Apostle Paul to assist him with his health so he could do his spiritual work. How long has it been since you have been to the doctor for a physical? Remember, *we may be saved, but we still live in a broken world.*

❓ Do you have unconfessed sin in your life?

Depression can also set in when there's sin in your life that needs to be dealt with. Confess it and ask God to help you overcome it. John 16:7-14 teaches us that the Holy Spirit is sent into the world to convict the world (including Christians) of sin, of righteousness, and of judgment. Please remember, the Lord won't condone in the life of the Christian what He condemns in the life of the non-Christian. If you are not a Christian, your guilt comes from God working in your life to help you turn to

Him. If you are a Christian, the guilt is a gift from God to you so you can find the sweet relief and peace that comes with His forgiveness (1 John 1:9).

❓ Is your life plagued by broken relationships?

Is there someone you have wronged?

Matthew 5:23-24 (NLT) tells us to go to them and seek forgiveness.

> *23 So if you are standing before the altar in the Temple, offering a sacrifice to God, and you suddenly remember that someone has something against you, 24 leave your sacrifice there beside the altar. Go and be reconciled to that person. Then come and offer your sacrifice to God.*

Is there someone who has wronged you?

Matthew 18:15-17 (NLT) tells us to go to them and gives us a prescription for restoring broken relationships.

> *15 If another believer sins against you, go privately and point out the fault. If the other person listens and confesses it, you have won that person back. 16 But if you are unsuccessful, take one or two others with you and go back again, so that everything you say may be confirmed by two or three witnesses. 17 If that person still refuses to listen, take your case to the church. If the church decides you are right, but the other person won't accept it, treat that person as a pagan or a corrupt tax collector.*

❓ Have you given in to "Stinking Thinking"?

In this world of pressures, failures, broken dreams, and sin, it's easy to get caught up in the cycle of "stinking thinking" instead of having an "attitude of gratitude." The Apostle Paul, writing from a Roman jail (Phil 4:4-9, NLT), implores us to keep our eyes on things that are good and lovely.

> *4 Always be full of joy in the Lord. I say it again — rejoice! 5 Let everyone see that you are considerate in all you do. Remember, the Lord is coming soon. 6 Don't worry about anything; instead, pray about everything. Tell God what you need, and thank him for all he has done. 7 If you do this, you will experience God's peace, which is far more wonderful than the human mind can understand. His peace will guard your hearts and minds as you live in Christ Jesus. 8 And now, dear brothers and sisters, let me say one more thing as I close this letter. Fix your thoughts on what is true and honorable and right. Think about things that are pure and lovely and admirable. Think about things that are excellent and worthy of praise. 9 Keep putting into practice all you learned from me and heard from me and saw me doing, and the God of peace will be with you.*

Paul tells us that everyone has a "good list" and a "bad list." When someone asks us, "How are you doing?" we have to choose which list we are going to talk about.

When I am tired or empty, it's easy to get my eyes off of my "good list" and only think about the "bad list." For me, the "bad list" *is* me: my failures, my hurts, and my feelings. I frankly get sick of *me*!

Whether we are in a Roman jail, in a poverty-stricken city called Philippi, or living in a mansion, when we begin to only see the bad things in our lives, we fall prey to depression. Paul's counsel to all of us living on the edge of despair is to stop and take a look at the "good list." When we focus on the blessings and recall how God has kept His word in the past through healing, help, and comfort, we can face our future with confidence.

❓ Who are you using for counselors?

Too often depression deepens when we look for counselors who merely agree with us. We *want* someone to take our side, understand our anger or hurt, and help us feel justified. But we *need* to measure the counselors and their counsel by Scripture. Consider James 1:2-7; 3:17-18; and 1 Corinthians 6:1-4.

❓ Are you isolating yourself from the people you need?

When depression attacks, we often withdraw from the very people we need most. We want to separate ourselves from people, circumstances, or relationships, fearing they'll only bring more pressure into our lives. Hebrews 3:12-13 (NASB) warns us to

> take care, brethren, lest there should be in any one of you an evil, unbelieving heart, in falling away from the living God. But encourage one another day after day, as long as it is still called 'Today,' lest any one of you be hardened by the deceitfulness of sin.

How Can We Overcome Depression?

When depression crowds into my nights, I've found comfort in hiding the Psalms in my heart and reflecting on them during the long nights that depression brings. *"I have hidden your word in my heart that I might not sin against you"* (Ps 119:11). It sure helps me to focus on the "good list."

David, the writer of most of the Psalms, was a man who also faced times of great depression. As I read his writings, I discover someone else who understands my feelings. Not only did David understand, but he gives me a prescription for climbing out of the pit of despair. He was a son forgotten by his physical dad, a rejected brother, and an overachiever who was envied and hunted down by his beloved king.

His best friend died. He experienced a broken marriage, had an affair, and murdered a close friend to cover his own sin. He watched his children rebel, sin, and die. He built a great kingdom, but lost every meaningful relationship. Is it any wonder that David, a great soldier, at times turned into a depressed coward? In Psalm 139 David reflects on the lessons he's learned. (We are always smarter when looking back than when we are in the middle of the battle.)

God is always there, and He always knows.

♦ Psalm 139:1-6 (NLT): *¹O LORD, you have examined my heart and know every-thing about me. ²You know when I sit down or stand up. You know my every thought when far away. ³You chart the path ahead of me and tell me where to stop and rest. Every moment you know where I am. ⁴You know what I am going to say even before I say it, LORD. ⁵You both precede and follow me. You place your hand of blessing on my head. ⁶Such knowledge is too wonderful for me, too great for me to know!*

We can never run away from God.

♦ Psalm 139:7-12 (NLT): *⁷I can never escape from your spirit! I can never get away from your presence! ⁸If I go up to heaven, you are there; if I go down to the place of the dead, you are there. ⁹If I ride the wings of the morning, if I dwell by the farthest oceans, ¹⁰even there your hand will guide me, and your strength will support me. ¹¹I could ask the darkness to hide me and the light around me to become night— ¹²but even in darkness I cannot hide from you.*

God has a plan for every life.

♦ Psalm 139:13-18 (NLT): *¹³You made all the delicate, inner parts of my body and knit me together in my mother's womb. ¹⁴Thank you for making me so wonderfully com-plex! Your workmanship is marvelous—and how well I know it. ¹⁵You watched me as I was being formed in utter seclusion, as I was woven together in the dark of the womb. ¹⁶You saw me before I was born. Every day of my life was recorded in your book. Every moment was laid out before a single day had passed. ¹⁷How precious are your thoughts about me, O God! They are innumerable! ¹⁸I can't even count them; they outnumber the grains of sand! And when I wake up in the morning you are still with me!*

God knows who our enemies are.

♦ Psalm 139:19-22 (NLT): *¹⁹O God, if only you would destroy the wicked! Get out of my life, you murderers! ²⁰They blaspheme you; your enemies take your name in vain. ²¹O LORD, shouldn't I hate those who hate you? Shouldn't I despise those who resist you? ²²Yes, I hate them with complete hatred for your enemies are my enemies.*

God gives us directions on how to be restored to himself.

♦ Psalm 139:23-24 (NLT): *²³Search me, O God, and know my heart; test me and know my thoughts. ²⁴Point out anything in me that offends you, and lead me along the path of everlasting life.*

As long as there is God . . . there is hope!

If I ask you, "How are you?" which "list" are you going to tell me about? Will it be "stinking thinking" or an "attitude of gratitude"? It's your choice!

Practical Application

1. **Take "inventory."** Could your depression be from one of the main causes I've listed in this chapter?
2. **Quit trying to "fix" the symptoms.** Focus on the real issue (your health, a broken relationship, sin, etc.).
3. **Pray.** Ask God to help you—to show you what you need to do, or *not* do. Ask Him to remind you of the good things in your life.
4. **Read.** Feed your mind on His Word. Perhaps you'll find comfort in Psalms too!
5. **Worship.** Take time to praise the Lord—and to listen.
6. **Rest.** Do you need to cancel some responsibilities this week or call people to take your place? Remember, you are not the only soldier in God's army.
7. **Connect with other Christians.** Don't isolate! Do you need to seek out a Christian who will help you think through and process, who will advise and encourage you?
   - Who should it be?
   - Can it be by phone?
   - If you communicate best in writing, could it be done through e-mails or letters?
8. **Get moving.** Do a project that brings you closer to God and helps you feel productive. For me, it's writing. Nothing directs my life more than sitting down, being quiet, thinking, and then writing to God. I know a woman who draws close to God when she paints. Still, there are folks that enjoy quiet walks with God. Although we shouldn't just "get busy for busy's sake," it's important not to just sit around when we get down. Find something that suits you and allows God to speak to your heart.

This is not some magical formula to cure depression, but rather, it is a process to help you draw close to God in your times of darkness.

Dear Family and Friends,

Have I told you of my "athletic career"? In the fifth grade I made it to the marbles championship match, and I lost to a girl!

Football wasn't much better. I weighed 130 pounds in my uniform and shoes; I was small and slow, but I really wanted to play. At one game I made the first two tackles of the game, but then I was taken out of the game because of a cut over my eye. In another game a giant of a kid didn't even blink when he ran over me as I attempted to block on a pass play. I remember the game we played at a school with kids who had broken the law. On one play, I ran the ball hard, stepping on one kid and tripping over another. I thought I was going to run into the end zone and be a hero, but instead I fell down. As it turned out, both of my "fallen" opponents had a broken leg. During that game a <u>very</u> large kid decided to beat me up—right there on the field! At the end of the game the other team lost 21 to 20. They were really angry, and I thought they were going to kill me. More than ten people were waiting at the door to take me down. Being a real "hero," I was hiding in the locker room—scared to death! The coach went to the bus and told the rest of the team to go back into the locker room. He said to me, "Putman, you get in the middle of the team as we walk out, and look innocent!"

Did I tell you I received a first place in the pole vault? I was the only one entered. Did I tell you I took a third place in the mile? You've got it now . . . there were only three of us competing. So much for my dreams of being a great athlete!

Sometimes you can do _your_ best, but because it wasn't _the_ best, your dreams don't come true. Other times you get what you hoped for, but it still doesn't satisfy you. Did I tell you that in high school I was chosen the vice president of the student body, or that I had played the main character in two plays? Did you know that I was selected "Boy of the Year" by the students and received the "Citizenship Award" by the teachers? Did I ever tell you that even when I reached these goals, I still wasn't satisfied? In fact many of my "accomplishments" in life have left me unsatisfied. I've discovered that if I don't have the right goals, and if I don't let Jesus help me, I'm just never satisfied with the results.

What do you do when you do _your_ best, but it isn't _the_ best? What do you do when you do succeed, you reach the top of the ladder, accomplish your goals, and get everything you hoped for, but it's just not enough? Maybe chapter nine will help.

Thanks for reading. I love you.
Dad/Grandpa/Bill

CHAPTER NINE

When Your Accomplishments Don't Satisfy

A Message for Driven People: It Matters Who's Driving!

Confessions of a Prodigal

Have you been successful, but at the wrong things? Are you good at things that really don't matter or don't last? Have you tried to be a Christian, but failed? Have you turned your energies toward other things? Are you trying really hard? Are you tired? You're probably a prodigal—looking for something, anything, that will satisfy.

The Story of a Successful Failure

A man had a wife and two sons. The father took from his earnings and purchased a house and clothes for the boys to wear. He paid for their schooling and college and convinced himself he was doing right by his wife and sons. Still, the sons said to their father, "Father, please give us some of your time. Please play with us, listen to us, and help us know that we are loved. Please be a daddy and a dad to us." But their father was a very busy man.

And for many days, the father would journey into the far country. He gathered up all his personal dreams and interests and poured his time into his work, responsibilities, and invest-ments. He spent his extra time with friends, chased his hobbies, and played with his latest toy. He spent more and more time away from his family, until his home was not his own.

When the man had spent all his energy and riches on things that wouldn't satisfy and with company who were not really friends, a famine settled in his heart. He began to long for a "home," true friends, and a real companion. He ached for children and grandchildren with whom he could share his life.

And when he finally came to his senses, he said to himself, "Others have found true happiness with their wives and their children, but I am here, empty and alone. I will return to my wife and children and say, 'I have sinned against you and God. I have become so terribly distracted. Please forgive me. I am no longer worthy to be called your husband or your dad. Please let me return as a servant to meet your needs.'"

And so he set out to return to his home. When his wife and youngest son saw his repentant heart, they were filled with love and compassion and embraced him. And before he could fully explain, his wife and son exclaimed, "Quick! Let's welcome Dad. It's time to celebrate! Let's have a party." And so the party began.

Meanwhile, the older son was away at work. When he heard that his father had returned and that his mother and brother were giving him a party, he was amazed. "Why are you welcoming him back?" He questioned them. "He was never there for us. He squandered his money and time, chasing after his own ambitions! Yet you are giving him a party and delight in his return? If I were in charge, I'd make his life miserable!"

And his mother and brother said, "We had to celebrate this happy day. For your father was dead and has come back to life! He was lost, but now is found."

—Bill Putman, August 9, 2004
(A modern day parable adapted from Luke 15:11-24)

What Happened?

A dear friend of mine has been doing a fine job "running the race," but now he has failed God, himself, his family, and church. He lies panting, broken in faith and spirit, on the sidelines. As my heart aches for him, I wonder, "What happened?"

Did he take his eyes off of the Lord Jesus and place his eyes on the world's empty promises? Did he take his eyes off of his commitments to his wife and children and become weary of marriage, family, and responsibilities? Did he get caught up in the trap of self-satisfaction and instant gratification? What would lead this man to the choices he made, choices that wounded him, and those who love him, with memories that can never go away this side of heaven? Did he climb to the top of the "ladder to success" only to discover that his ladder was leaning against the wrong wall? Did he spend all his energy on himself, his job, and his children so there was nothing left for his marriage or his relationship with God? Did he do all the "right things" for the wrong reasons: popularity, financial success, friendships, or admiration? Did he reach middle age and discovered that either his dreams didn't come true, or if they did, they didn't bring any satisfaction?

Has My Friend Missed the Warning Lights and Danger Signs?

I love him, but as I've watched his life and values unravel, I'm afraid for him. Is my friend heading for some of the same miserable mistakes I made in my life? I've had to learn the hard way that sometimes Satan's lies sound really logical, and tired people can be deceived easily!

My Story

> **Satan's Lie:**
> **"Hard Work + Success = Approval and Satisfaction."**

As a teenager I remember my dad saying many times, "There has never been a lazy Putman." Because I desperately wanted to gain his approval, I listened. "All you have to do to be successful is work five percent more than anyone around you." I thought, "If five percent will get me his approval and make me successful, then I'll work twenty percent harder!" The truth is, even though I was successful in the jobs I had, working hard didn't produce joy in me; it wasn't satisfying. I decided there had to be more to life than "success."

> **Satan's Lie:**
> **"Hard Work + Success + A Mission =**
> **Approval and Satisfaction."**

At the age of 21, I accepted Jesus as my Savior and started training for the ministry. I made a brand and marked all my books with it: **AAA–0.** Anything, Anywhere, Anytime –(bar) **0** (nothing). I wanted to serve the Lord always, holding nothing back. I was a hard worker with a brand, a mission statement! But it wasn't enough. I still didn't get the approval I desperately needed to feel good about myself and my life. I had no joy, no satisfaction. I was more like a dead Christmas tree with the lights carefully arranged, than a living apple tree abundant with lasting fruit.

> ### Satan's Lie:
> ### "Hard Work + Success + A Mission + Getting Organized = Approval and Satisfaction."

When I was 36, my life was so busy it was hard to think. The children were ages 12, 11, 9, 8, and 6. I moved from being a senior pastor of one church to leading a church planting organization with *several* ministry responsibilities. I worked hard at AAA–0, and I was focused, but nothing I accomplished brought me satisfaction and joy. I was sure I was still missing something, and Satan was ready to fill in the blanks.

From my journal, 1975:

I'm working hard and I'm committed. I just have to get organized! Let's see. Everyone has time: 86,400 seconds every day. Every day has 1440 minutes and twenty-four hours. There are seven days in a week and fifty-two weeks in every year—and I have an unknown number of years!

I have just read somewhere, "You are like an onion—the layers of your life make up the sum total of who you are, and if you fail on one layer, it will ruin all the other layers." I conclude: I need to identify everything that is expected of me so I don't leave any of the important things out. I will write down these different "layers" of expectations, including the different responsibilities I have for each layer.

My list looked something like this:

> I am Bill Putman, child of God. As such, there are 12 essentials I must do . . .
> I am Bill Putman, Bobbi's husband. As such, there are 22 essentials I must do . . .
> I am Bill Putman, father of five. As such, there are 23 essentials I must do . . .
> I am Bill Putman, a person. As such, there are 14 essentials I must do . . .
> I am Bill Putman, Executive Director of a church planting organization. As such, there are 41 essentials I must do.

> I am Bill Putman, founding minister of a new church. As such, there are 25 essentials I must do . . .
> I am Bill Putman, son, son-in-law, brother, and uncle. As such, there are 7 essentials I must do.
> I am Bill Putman, friend. As such, there are 22 essential relationships I must maintain . . .
> Let's see, 12 plus 22 plus 23 plus 14 plus 41 plus 25 plus 7 plus 22 equals _166_ absolute essentials that I must do or I will fail!

Those years of my life were so busy I almost crowded God and my family out. I was driven by the immediate and not the eternal. I was ruled by my schedule and an alarm wristwatch. I actually thought I didn't need as much sleep as everyone else (another lie!), so I added 5:00 am to 8:00 am to my already long day with normal work weeks averaging 75 plus hours a week! I thought taking a few hours off was all right instead of taking days off. I remember taking one of my two vacation weeks a year to do a revival meeting so I'd have extra money to pay doctor bills or to buy bikes for my children. Looking back, I was driven, but the wrong person was driving . . . me!

The *result* of believing the lies: *I wasn't there for my own wife and family.* The truth hurts. I did a better job on other peoples' families than I did my own, and our home turned into a house. I was a stranger to my family. I was doing many things for God, but I wasn't doing anything *with* Him.

I had identified what I expected of me, and I had the audacity to attempt them all! But they were *my* expectations, not God's. It's no wonder that I nearly lost my faith, marriage, children, and health! I started measuring my success in terms of hours worked and the number of things I crossed off my daily to-do list, instead of being a maturing Christian and nurturing husband and father. Because of the hours of work and my endless lists, I had the false sense that I was getting my job done and accomplishing many things, but the cancer of distance, weariness, and loneliness were eating at my life and our home. I was a hard worker with a mission who became organized and then fell apart!

Doing It My Way!

Not long ago, I used my Essentials List from my journal in a sermon. As I started reading the list I stood confidently. Continuing to read, I walked over to a chair and sat down. Reading on, I slouched in the chair and eventually slumped to the floor. At last, when I finished the list, I lay flat on my back, and with a whisper said, "Where do I go to resign?!"

To say the least, I was not satisfied and there was very little joy in my life. I was completely run down and "ripe" for Satan's biggest lie yet.

Do you believe that Jesus is your Savior, but act like it's your job to stay saved?

Warning: Tired Person Ahead!

> **Satan's Lie:**
> **"Give Up . . . You'll Never Be Satisfied."**

At age 40 I was so tired I secretly gave up—marriage, parenting, church, and Christianity. There was no joy, no satisfaction. I had worked hard, focused on the mission, experienced a lot of success, gained a fair amount of approval (at least from outsiders!), and gotten organized. I chased so many noble things! I did my best—only to end up "dead" and "lost." Running this race wasn't easy. It wasn't difficult. It was impossible! I bought the lie and wanted out!!

I asked God to take my life. He didn't.

I was tempted to be immoral. I wanted to, but I couldn't.

I tried to get everyone in my world to change. They wouldn't.

I wanted to give my family away. No one wanted them.

I finally just started going through the motions in my ministry.

I gave up reading the Bible for myself and began "borrowing" sermons from others. (It was sort of like carrying water from someone else's well.)

I faced one crisis after another in my marriage and with my children.

I gave up on the inside, but God and my wife wouldn't give up on me.

Finding the Truth!

When I was 45 I finally realized I needed to let the Lord do the driving! I was going under, spiritually and emotionally. My life was full of crises and I had given up. What I needed was to have the Lord weed away all the important in my life and just leave the eternal.

The Parable of the Branch

Hello! I'm a branch, and I've got real problems. If I don't produce any fruit, the gardener is going to cut me off and throw me into the fire to burn! Even if I do produce fruit, the gardener is going to prune me! Does that seem fair to you?

Well, I'd better get started producing some fruit. There's a lot to worry about; it's complicated! There are a lot of things that need to be done. I've got to worry about whether the sun will shine, if there will be enough rain. I've got to worry about the mineral content in the soil, weeds, bugs, and diseases. I've got to be sure the vine sends me nutrients and my branches grow plenty of leaves. That's a lot to keep track of!

"Come on fruit! Where are you? Fruit, in the Name of Jesus, I command you to grow!" Man, this takes longer than I thought! I still don't see any fruit. Oh no! I hear the gardener coming. I can see Him walking down my row! Are those clippers he's holding? No, thank goodness. He only has that stupid pesticide spray; I hate the smell of it. But, wait! He's checking to see if I've produced any fruit yet. Now I know I'm in trouble!

"No! What are you doing? Don't do that! I like my stems where they are; I like the shade down by the ground. Why are you tying me to that wire up where the sun will make me hot?"

Oh man, am I relieved. The gardener left, and He didn't clip me. But, now I'm all exposed . . . and baking in the hot sun! I can see all those other branches around me growing fruit. What am I doing wrong?

Wait a minute, is that **my** fruit I see? It is! "Hey everybody, see my fruit! I'm growing! Look at me! Wahoo!" I'm not just a great branch, I'm fantastic! I'll bet mine is the best fruit around! I love my fruit! Wait a minute. "Gardener, what are you doing? Stop! Don't take my fruit!" Why did He take away my fruit? Wait a second. Now what's He doing? I don't like the look of this. "Stop! You already took my fruit. Ouch! Pruning hurts! Do You even know what you're doing?"

Just look at me. How humiliating! I'm so embarrassed. I've been cut back to nearly nothing.

What Do You Do When You've Been Pruned?

When we are "pruned" we need to remember 1 John 4:4, "*Greater is He that is in you than He that is in the world!*" and Philippians 4:13, "*I can do all things through Christ who strengthens me!*" When I read this, something begins to stir inside me. Think of it; our hope is in Jesus! I think of the words of John 1:1-3, *"All things were made through Him!"* and John 1:14, *"and He became flesh and dwelt among us."* That's it! Jesus: born of a virgin, able to do miracles (He made the lame to walk, the blind to see, and raised the dead!), faced every temptation, remained sinless, taught us marvelous truths, and conquered death!

I remember being asked to preach at a conference, and I was given the subject: "YES, WE CAN!" The irony of it! As I prepared the message, I thought, "YES, WE CAN? Listen, guys, I tried and failed. Don't count on me!" I thought, "I've looked at our team. If it's just you and me, we are in REAL trouble!"

As I prepared and preached that message, the Lord convicted me. I decided I had to change brands. **AAA–0**, Anything, Anywhere, Anytime bar **0** (nothing) had placed all the responsibility for action on myself! That night I asked the Lord to add to my brand. I changed brands to **AAA–0 + Philippians 4:13.** (I can do Anything, Anywhere, Anytime . . . **BAR NOTHING** . . . **"through Christ who gives me strength."**) That doesn't mean I keep trying to accomplish everything on my "essentials list" and add "a little Christ." All I have to do is "remain in Him."

♦ John 15:1-17 (NLT): *I am the true vine, and my Father is the gardener. He cuts off every branch that doesn't produce fruit, and he prunes the branches that do bear fruit so they will produce even more. You have already been pruned for greater fruitfulness by the message I have given you. Remain in me, and I will remain in you. For a branch cannot produce fruit if it is severed from the vine, and you cannot be fruitful apart from me. Yes, I am the vine; you are the branches. Those who remain in me and I in them, will produce much fruit. For apart from me you can do nothing. Anyone who parts from me is thrown away like a useless branch and withers. Such branches are gathered into a pile to be burned. But if you stay joined to me and my words remain in you, you may ask any request you like, and it will be granted! My true disciples produce much fruit. This brings great glory to my Father. I have loved you even as the Father has loved me. Remain in my love. When you obey me, you remain in my love, just as I obey my Father and remain in his love. I have told you this so that you will be filled with my joy. Yes, your joy will overflow! I command you to love each other in the same way that I love you. And here is how to measure it — the greatest love is shown when people lay down their lives for their friends. You are my friends if you obey me. I no longer call you servants, because a master doesn't confide in his servants. Now you are my friends, since I have told you everything the Father told me. You didn't choose me. I chose you. I appointed you to go and produce fruit that will last, so that the Father will give you whatever you ask for, using my name. I command you to love each other.*

Do you see the list? I'm supposed to trust the Lord, produce lasting fruit, be full of joy, obey Him, love other Christians, and be willing to lay down my life for them . . . but, not in my own strength. My only job is to *abide in the vine.* It actually says that seven times in six verses! My Father, God, is the gardener, and knows what I need. Jesus is the vine and will supply all I need. All I'm called to do is stay attached to Jesus, remain in Him, *let Him do His work through me!* And He promises joy . . . that overflows! What a relief.

As I think of my life (now I'm 64), I have always tried to gain approval and acceptance by how hard I work. I thought success would bring me satisfaction. I thought if I just kept trying, working out the kinks and fine tuning my lists, I'd finally get it right. The less my plans worked, the harder *I* worked, and the farther I got from God's "essentials list." As it turned out, he never wanted me to work that hard, no matter how noble the task.

I am still struggling to trust the Lord to work through me, and I so often "try to help" Him. Letting go is humbling, but I'm trying to remember:

> *Everything in my life is not my responsibility*
> *. . . but my response to God's ability!*

My Prayer

Lord, I started this letter thinking about my friend and ended up thinking about how faithful You are. I'm sorry that I've depended so much on me and so little on you through the years. I was lost, but now I'm found!

Lord, I'm so grateful that even though I'm 64, and, in most people's eyes, "old enough to know better," You still see me as "little Billy." Just like a child, I often run ahead of You and try to grow my own fruit. When I tire or fall down and cry, You pick me up, dry my tears, and carry me for a while. Thanks for caring. Thanks for carrying me. I love You, Lord.

Little Billy Putman.

Dear Family and Friends,

I heard one of my mentors once say to a class of prospective ministers, "I don't care how homely you are. If there is a desire in your heart for immorality, Satan will bring the opportunity."

Did you know that there was a time in my life when I had to battle for a pure thought life, not just daily or hourly, but minute by minute? I believe we all face this to some degree. I can still remember when I was a child and my dad bumped into the car in front of us because he was distracted looking at a woman in short shorts!

I want to write today about the crisis of facing moral temptations. I can just see my daughter Melody putting her hands over her ears and saying, "That's more than I wanted to know!" It may be more than you wanted to know, but I believe the information in this chapter is material all of us need to know. _You_ will face temptation. _You_ will have to fight the battle for your mind—your imagination! _You_ will face having to make a choice of your actions, and if you fail, _you_ will have to learn how to let the Lord change your habits and give you victory.

Thanks for reading. I'm praying for you as you fight the fight for purity!

Dad/Grandpa/Bill

CHAPTER TEN

When You Are Tempted to Be Immoral

Caution! Danger! Sexual Temptation Ahead.

She walked into my office and said, "I've decided to have an affair." I started to say, "Oh, I'm so sorry," but she interrupted me and said, "And I decided to have the affair with you!"

I was vulnerable; there were many pressures in my life. I was working too hard at church and spending too little time with my wife. I was feeling fat and forty, over the hill, and unattractive. She was attractive and unhappily married. When she offered herself to me, I knew I was in trouble.

For a few moments it was almost like time stood still. In my mind, I picked up my "imagination remote control." I pushed fast forward, and in a moment, I was involved in an imaginary intimate embrace.

What did I choose to do? You'll have to read the end of the chapter to know what happened.

It Seems Like We Live in the Middle of a Sexual War!

Have you noticed that Hollywood and television like to make sin look good? They always glamorize relationships so the hours of flirtation and climax look so appealing. Seductive commercials try to lure us into buying anything from cars to chewing gum to window cleaner! Even during an innocent trip to the local department store we're confronted with bigger than life pictures of women in lingerie. Living together before you're married is considered culturally acceptable, promoted by many and openly celebrated as "the next step" in a "normal" relationship. Yet God teaches us differently. There's no doubt, we're in a battle for our purity *and* our children's.

Even the great moral lessons of the Bible are often perverted into Hollywood fantasies.

If Hollywood made a movie about David and Bathsheba, the producers would probably pick out one section from their life to really exploit. They would fast-forward beyond David's victories and show David looking from his rooftop garden to see Bathsheba bathing. They again would fast-forward to the scene of their intimate embrace. The music would capture our imagination and the camera would zoom in so we could feel their passion.

The story doesn't end there though. We can't let Hollywood capture our imagination, causing us to rewind and replay—rewind and replay—the moments of passion. The Holy Spirit can help us fast-forward to when David desperately tries to cover up their sin by deceit and murder. Fast-forward to the death of their baby, the incest and rape of David's daughter Tamar, the death of his son Absalom, and the repeated moral failures of their son Solomon. Fast-forward to see their grandchildren rebel and God ultimately withdraw His blessing and protection from the whole nation. But this is the "down" part of the story, and our enemy doesn't want us to face the harsh reality of sin's consequences.

Moral Failure Has Consequences

I don't know about you, but when I face temptation I don't want to think about the consequences. Moral failure is all around us, and the consequences are real and usually devastating. Several of my close friends have been immoral. Their brokenhearted families are left wounded and disillusioned.

Many parents have told me they've discovered their sons or daughters are sexually active. Just two weeks ago a friend called shocked, disappointed, and scared. He shared that his fourteen-year-old daughter had given away her virginity. Another parent shared that her very young daughter had been giving oral sex to her boyfriend. Another called weeping; his teenage daughter is pregnant. Yet another called and announced that his child has told him he's a homosexual.

The moral crisis around us that brings us difficult decisions also often victimizes our most innocent. Recently three more families I know have discovered that one or more of their children are being molested. Last summer, in our community, three people were brutally murdered as a molester captured his "prey." Two kidnapped children were molested before one of them was also murdered. I realize that not all sexual sin leads to murder or molestation, but all sins bring consequences.

♦ Galatians 6:7-8 (NLT): *⁷Don't be misled. Remember that you can't ignore God and get away with it. You will always reap what you sow! ⁸Those who live only to satisfy their own sinful desires will harvest the consequences of decay and death.*

How Are You Handling Your Temptations?

It's not wrong to be tempted, but how we handle those temptations will determine whether we sin or not. So, how are you doing? Let's take a closer look.

- Have you caught yourselves looking too deeply into someone's eyes and wondering "what if?"
- Have you found yourself wondering what she'd look like in tight fitting jeans or caught yourself looking for the hint of a thigh or a breast?
- Has that friendly hug lasted too long?
- Have you been innocently "flirting" with someone else's mate when you suddenly realized that somewhere you stopped flirting and longed to go further?
- Have you been surfing the Internet when suddenly a picture captured your attention for just a moment, you stopped to stare, and then you let your imagination run wild?
- Have you been reminded of an improper past sexual experience and then caught yourself using the "rewind button," of your memory to play scenes from your past over and over again?
- Have you met face to face with someone that you shared intimately with in the past, and your inflated memory seems better than your present reality?
- Have you been using your "imagination remote control" to play with your sexual imagination, indulging in inappropriate fantasies?
- Do you enjoy the temptation, the thrill of "flying close to the flame" or "driving close to the edge" or "almost but not quite"?

Beware! All these behaviors are ***very dangerous***. If you begin to play the "what it would be like" game, you may find yourself wanting it to be real . . . and then "the game" will end.

A Note for Those Who Think "This Will Never Happen to Me."

Maybe there are some of you who would try to convince me that you've never thought of being unfaithful, read a book with explicit sexual descriptions, or watched a movie with inappropriate scenes, and never wondered "what it would be like to be that person" or "to have that experience." Maybe you concluded that "you will never be tempted" or that "good parenting and home schooling will protect your children!" Have you forgotten that the Bible says, *"Remember, temptations that come into your life are no different from what others experience"* (1 Cor 10:13). Everyone will be tempted!

A Note for Those Who Have Failed.

We all face temptation, and we all will lose some battles. First John 1:9 tells us *"If we confess our sins, he is faithful and just to forgive us our sins, and to cleanse us from all unrighteousness."* We confess . . . He forgives. His forgiveness does not mean the consequences will magically disappear, though. He forgives *and* helps us deal with the bondage and consequences of sin. David took his failure to God and asked Him to cleanse him. He made no excuses and accepted God's sovereign judgment.

> ◆ Psalm 51:1-19 (NLT): *[1]Have mercy on me, O God, because of your unfailing love. Because of your great compassion, blot out the stain of my sins. [2]Wash me clean from my guilt. Purify me from my sin. [3]For I recognize my shameful deeds — they haunt me day and night. [4]Against you, and you alone, have I sinned; I have done what is evil in your sight. You will be proved right in what you say, and your judgment against me is just.*

Maybe some of you have experienced one failure after another and want to give up. Maybe you have formed destructive sexual habits or addictions. There is hope. Keep reading.

Preparing for Battle

The battle for our moral purity is, in many ways, like any other battle we face as Christians. We should plan, in our times of strength, for our times of weakness. Good planning and prevention often head off disaster. Let's look at it one step at a time.

Look for the Lies

Identify any lies you've started believing. Before you can control your actions, you need to "take captive every thought." Replace the lies with Truth. Are you believing a lie?

- Maybe one of your friends has fallen in his or her temptations and you've thought, "If he can't make marriage work, there's no hope for me," or, "If she can't be pure, I know I can't." **Those are lies!**
- Maybe you've started listening to our culture and found yourself compromising. "No one will find out." "It's only flirtation; it won't lead anywhere." "It's OK as long as no one gets hurt." "It's not really wrong." "The Bible is old-fashioned." "Everyone is doing it." Or "Oh well, touching or oral sex isn't really sex." **They're all lies!**
- Maybe you thought, "I haven't felt this excited for years!" "My mate [husband or wife] doesn't make me feel like this person does," or "If it feels this good, it can't be wrong." **More lies!**
- Worse yet, maybe you've thought, "I've prayed, and I know God doesn't want me to be unhappy," or "I've prayed, 'Lord if you don't want me to be in this relationship, *You* take them away.'" **More lies!**

In the Middle of All the Lies We Need to Listen to God's Truth!

I love how God uses the Apostle Paul to both warn us and give us hope. We *will* be tempted. First Corinthians 10:13 (NLT) says, *"The temptations that come into your life are no different from what others experience."* In the middle of our temptations, "God will be faithful." When it seems like the temptations are so severe that there is no hope for me, the Scripture says, *"God is faithful. He will keep the temptation from becoming so strong that you can't stand up against it. When you are tempted, he will show you a way out so you will not give in to it."*

➤ Are you looking at your various temptations, or are you looking to your God who promises to give you a way of escape?

➤ Are you reading, memorizing, and claiming God's word to help you in temptation? (Ps 119:11).

➤ How are you responding to the work of the Holy Spirit in your life? The Lord promises to send Him to us to convict us of sin (what we should not do), righteousness (what we should do), and the fact that we will stand before God who will judge our thoughts, actions, and habits?

➤ Are you focusing on the worries of temptation, pressures, or the immediate crisis and now are afraid? Are you counting the number of your enemies that surround you, or the number of your friends who are falling to temptations, or are you fixing your thoughts on what is true and honorable and right? Are you choosing to think about those things that are pure, lovely, and admirable? Are you concentrating your attention on negative things or on those things God gives you that are excellent and worthy of praise? (Phil 4:6-9).

➤ Are you trying to face your battles alone? Again Scripture gives us practical help when it warns us to stand together and be accountable to each other (Heb 3:12-15).

Don't Try to Ignore Your Weaknesses Because Satan Will Sneak Up on You!

Once you identify the lies, look for your areas of vulnerability. I don't know how Satan dresses up when he comes to tempt you, but I know he uses our selfishness and our human appetite to fill the vacuum in our hearts with anything *but* God. What toys does he dangle in front of you? Cars, boats, houses, or even security? When Satan comes to you, is it through a desire for wealth, power, sex, or vengeance? Does he lure you with excitement or adventure? Where do you willingly compromise? Does boredom lead you to immoral thoughts? Does sexual curiosity lead you to Internet pornography? Does a longing to recapture your youth lead you to immoral fantasies? When you know where you're weak, you can begin to prepare your defenses.

♦ 1 Corinthians 6:9-20 (NLT)

⁹*Don't you know that those who do wrong will have no share in the Kingdom of God? Don't fool yourselves. Those who indulge in sexual sin, who are idol worshipers, adulterers, male prostitutes, homosexuals,* ¹⁰*thieves, greedy people, drunkards, abusers, and swindlers—none of these will have a share in the Kingdom of God.* ¹¹*There was a time when some of you were just like that, but now your sins have been washed away, and you have been set apart for God. You have been made right with God because of what the Lord Jesus Christ and the Spirit of our God have done for you.*

¹²*You may say, "I am allowed to do anything." But I reply, "Not everything is good for you." And even though "I am allowed to do anything," I must not become a slave to anything.* ¹³*You say, "Food is for the stomach, and the stomach is for food." This is true, though someday God will do away with both of them. But our bodies were not made for sexual immorality. They were made for the Lord, and the Lord cares about our*

bodies. [14]And God will raise our bodies from the dead by his marvelous power, just as he raised our Lord from the dead. [15]Don't you realize that your bodies are actually parts of Christ? Should a man take his body, which belongs to Christ, and join it to a prostitute? Never! [16]And don't you know that if a man joins himself to a prostitute, he becomes one body with her? For the Scriptures say, "The two are united into one." [17]But the person who is joined to the Lord becomes one spirit with him.

[18]Run away from sexual sin! No other sin so clearly affects the body as this one does. For sexual immorality is a sin against your own body. [19]Or don't you know that your body is the temple of the Holy Spirit, who lives in you and was given to you by God? You do not belong to yourself, [20]for God bought you with a high price. So you must honor God with your body.

Application—If You Are a Christian
1. Where you go, He goes.
2. What you do, He does.
3. How can I stay pure in a filthy world?

God Is God: He Is Everywhere, and You Can't Hide from Him!

I remember walking into a grocery store one day and noticing a leader from the church standing awkwardly at the magazine rack. He was holding a magazine sideways, obviously looking at the naked woman in the centerfold. I've always wondered, if he looked carefully to the left and then to the right, to see if he was being watched. I'll bet you he did. What he forgot to do is look *up*! God sees everything we think and do! David wrote:

♦ Psalm 139:1-2,7 (NLT): [1]O LORD, you have examined my heart and know everything about me. [2]You know when I sit down or stand up. You know my every thought when far away. . . . [7]I can never escape from your spirit! I can never get away from your presence.

God Is God: He Knows Everything and Will Judge Us.

♦ 1 Corinthians 6:9-10: [9]Don't you know that those who do wrong will have no share in the Kingdom of God? Don't fool yourselves. Those who indulge in sexual sin, who are idol worshipers, adulterers, male prostitutes, homosexuals, [10]thieves, greedy people, drunkards, abusers, and swindlers—none of these will have a share in the Kingdom of God.

In Job 31:1-12, we read that Job was the most righteous man of his generation, but he still faced sexual temptation. In order to be pure he wrote, "I made a covenant." Note the elements of his covenant with God:

1. He made a covenant with his eyes not to look with lust upon a young woman.
2. He made a covenant to remember that God judges the wicked.
3. He made a covenant to remember that God sees everything we think, see, or do and will judge us accurately.
   - He sees me if I stray from His pathway.
   - He sees when my heart lusts for something my eyes have seen.
   - He sees me when I am guilty of any other sin.
4. He made a covenant to remember that there is a price for all sin, but specific punishment for sexual sins.
   - Someone else will reap the financial benefit for all my work.
   - All my past work, like crops, will be uprooted.
   - My wife will belong to and sleep with another.
   - My sexual sins will be punished.
   - It will wipe out everything I own.

God Is God: There Is a Blessing Promised to Those Who Love Him and Keep His Commandments.

If a Christian is "one in whom Christ lives" (1 Cor 6:19-20) and if "greater is He that is in you than he that is in the world" (1 John 4:4), it's vital that Christians live every moment of their day as though they are living with their landlord. When I am tempted to thoughts I can't include the Lord in, I'm in danger.

Expect the Battle

Have you ever asked yourself why Christians have to battle so hard for moral purity? Shouldn't it be easier for us? After all, we're forgiven for our past, we've received the gift of the Holy Spirit, and we're going to heaven when we die. The Apostle Paul explains it this way:

- Galatians 5:17 (NLT): *The old sinful nature loves to do evil, which is just the opposite from what the Holy Spirit wants. And the Spirit gives us desires that are opposite from what the sinful nature desires. These two forces are constantly fighting each other, and your choices are never free from this conflict!*

I read of a missionary who was visiting with a new Christian about the pressures and temptations in his life. The young man said, "I feel like there is a battle in my heart between a black wolf and a white wolf." The missionary asked him, "Which wolf is going to win?" The young Christian said, "The one that I feed."

I read of a young man who called down from upstairs, "Mom, is this shirt I'm wearing dirty?" She responded, "Yes." The young man changed his shirt and went downstairs. He then asked, "How did you know it was dirty?" She said, "If it's doubtful, it's dirty."

If we look at the battle for our moral purity, we need to realize that sin takes place first in the head before it takes place in the bed (Matt 5:27). We need to realize that because the Lord lives in our lives, we don't have to fail. But the battle for moral purity is not just one battle, it is a war with a lifelong series of battles. Let me try to explain the war that is going on in every Christian's life.

A Parable about "IME"

I just got into a terrible fight. I hate that guy. I don't just dislike him, I hate him! His name is IME. He is really hard to be around. I've tried to get rid of him, but I can't.

*You ask, "What was the fight about?" Well, since I became a Christian, I've tried to convert IME. I spend a lot of time with him, but when we are together there is always a fight. It's all about **him**. It's **his** car; he's always angry when people get in **his** way. It's always **his** kids, **his** wife, and **his** job. I went to church last week with IME, and I couldn't even worship because IME was upset. People didn't treat **him** as **he** thought **he** deserved. They didn't sing the songs **he** liked, and the sermon didn't meet **his** need. No one went out of their way to make **him** feel welcome.*

*You should see old IME at **his** home. It's always "**all about IME**"—what **he** likes or doesn't like. It's all about **his** TV programs, what makes **him** happy or makes **him** mad. Even in **his** relationship with **his** wife, it's all about what satisfies **him**. I sure hate that guy. You ask, "Why don't you get rid of him, move away from him or something?" I did. I thought I'd even killed him once.*

By this time you probably figured out that IME's full name is I-ME-MY-MINE. The Scriptures call him selfishness, the flesh. He was a partner with Satan to keep me from heaven, and now, he partners with the world, the devil, and the flesh to steal my joy—to try to get me back again.

Since "IME" is also a relative of yours, I wanted to ask, how are you doing with IME? Have you noticed when you take your eyes off Jesus as your Savior and Lord, that you fall back into the same old battle with him? If you give old IME an inch, he takes a mile. If you open the door to temptation just a crack, IME crowds in and tries to overwhelm you, and soon, your heart and home are in bad shape all over again.

Be as alert as a soldier at war. Expect the attack, so you're not taken off guard.

Know Your Enemy and His Tactics

Our enemy is not flesh and blood but rather Satan and his team (Eph 6:12).

Satan has a "spy," a "betrayer," or an "undercover" agent in my life—old IME. He attacks through what we see, hear, feel, touch, and remember. Our battle with the enemy is progressive. If we win or lose a battle, there is always another battle in our future.

The first battleground is the **battle for control of our mind**.

If Satan can control our minds, he's got a shoe in the door and can take over the whole house! If I lose the battle for my mind, for what I think, for what I put into my mind—for biblical thinking—sin will creep into my mind. I will question Truth. If I lose the battle for what is real Truth, I will reject it and start believing the lies.

Let me illustrate. Which young man do you want to date your daughter? The one who still battles with Satan but is faithful to God in worship and prayer, reads his Bible and surrounds himself with good Christian friends? Or a young man who fills his mind with pornography, hangs out with the wrong crowd, and is uncomfortable with the things of God?

The battle for the mind never stops, and what we put into our minds and how we think about those things will determine how we face the second battlefield.

The second battlefield is **the battle for control of our actions**.

If our enemy controls our mind, it's pretty easy to control our behavior. Remember sexual sins occur in the head before they ever take place in the bed. If you are losing the battle for your mind, you will have to battle with thinking the wrong things, thinking the wrong words, thinking the wrong attitudes, and then seeing your thoughts break out into actions. Wrong thinking leads to wrong actions. Repeat the pattern enough times and you've formed a nasty habit, which leads us into the next battlefield.

The third battlefield is **the battle for control of our habits.**

If we lose the battle for our mind and lose the battle for our behavior, we will find ourselves addicted to, chained to, or bound to all sorts of undesirable habits. They may start out as flirtations with "the dark side," but somehow, day by day, week by week, they will take over, and Satan will control our habits.

If we lose the battle for our mind, actions, and habits we will begin to start thinking only of ourselves and our ambitions. We will eventually separate from Christians and divide from anyone who doesn't agree with us. We'll think everyone is wrong but us and become angry, jealous, and rebellious. We will even quit *trying* to control our attitudes, desires, actions, and addictions.

Winning the War

Jesus is always our example. When Satan tempted Him, He always looked to God. He used the "Sword of the Spirit," which is the Word of God, to fight the enemy (see Matthew 4). The Bible gives us instructions for our battle with Satan and old "IME."

♦ James 4:6-10 (NLT): *[6]He gives more and more strength to stand against such evil desires. As the Scriptures say, "God sets himself against the proud, but he shows favor to the humble." [7]So humble yourselves before God. Resist the Devil, and he will flee from you. [8]Draw close to God, and God will draw close to you. Wash your hands, you sinners; purify your hearts, you hypocrites. [9]Let there be tears for the wrong things you have done. Let there be sorrow and deep grief. Let there be sadness instead of laughter, and gloom instead of joy. [10]When you bow down before the Lord and admit your dependence on him, he will lift you up and give you honor.*

♦ 1 Corinthians 6:19-20 (NLT) says: *[19]Or don't you know that your body is the temple of the Holy Spirit who lives in you and was given to you by God? You do not belong to yourself, [20]for God bought you with a high price. So you must honor God with your body.*

Think of it; we ruined us. God washed us. God moved into us. We became His child, and we surrendered ownership of our own life, marriage, family—everything!

♦ Romans 12:1-2: *[1]Therefore I urge you, brothers, in view of God's mercy, to offer your bodies as living sacrifices, holy and pleasing to God—this is your spiritual act of worship. [2]Do not conform any longer to the pattern of this world, but be transformed by the renewing of your mind. Then you will be able to test and approve what God's will is — his good, pleasing and perfect will.*

Conclusion

I promised to share with you what I did when I heard her say, "I've decided to have an affair, and I've decided to have it with you."

I won't tell you the exact words I said, but in spite of what my "feelings" wanted to do, and because the Lord kept His promise to give me a way of escape, the battle plan (set into my mind *before* the temptation) came to my mind. I took out a piece of paper and said, "I'm sure I would enjoy sharing sexually with you, but before we do, I want to count what it would cost me." I wrote, "It will separate me from God. It would separate me from my wife and children. It would damage God's reputation in my life. I have to say no." I went on to say, "I can no longer be your pastor. Any help you get from this church will have to come through my wife." She said, "Well, I'll just go find someone else," and left. I sat there for a moment, called my wife Bobbi and told her the whole story. When I got to the part where I said any ministry she received would have to come through my wife, Bobbi said, "What am I supposed to do?" That week my wife took her to lunch. A few weeks later, it was my wife who went to the hospital after the woman was in a car wreck. More than ten years later she called and said, "Bill, I need help, you are the only man in my whole life that didn't use me."

What if I had given in to the temptation? God would have forgiven me, my marriage might have survived, but my wife and I would not have been able to reenter her life and help her through her crisis. I won that battle, but my war for a pure mind continues. How are you doing on your war?

Please pray for me. I'm able to be pure only because of Jesus.

Dear Family and Friends,

As I was writing this chapter, I read back in my journal and found the following letter. I don't remember who I was thinking about when I wrote it (I never sent it), but it could have been for any one of you. I hope as you read this material that you are doing well, but just in case you are going through a hard time, I hope you get a blessing from reading it.

Dear Child,

I've been watching and listening. I knew this time would probably come, even though I prayed it wouldn't. Your early days of being married are but a memory, and you've come to the place where you may be asking yourself, "What did I get into?"

One woman said, "When I got married I was looking for the ideal. It turned into an ordeal, and now I want a _new_ deal!" Do you feel that same way?

I've seen your looks of concern—the hurt in your face. I've heard the tension in your voice, and I believe you have come to understand what Mom and I learned a long time ago: It's hard to stay married.

The dreams you had—what your marriage was going to be—have become the nightmare of what it really is and you are wondering:

"Did I make a mistake? Marry the wrong person? Marry too young?"

"Is there someone else I would be happier with?"

"Should I have married at all?"

I'm glad you chose to be married! I know marriage is a risky venture. Most marriages end with divorce, and too many who stay married are walking wounded. Here's what I hope: I hope you will let the Lord help you be strong enough to stay married through the tough times and discover what your mom and I have found.

I'm praying for you. If there is anything I can do to help, please ask. I love you.

Dad/Grandpa/Bill

CHAPTER ELEVEN

When It's Hard to Stay Married

Do You Remember When Your Love Was Fresh and Alive?

Do you remember the excitement of first love? In the beginning it was like the crashing of two rivers meeting. You were drawn to each other and experienced a *face-to-face* intimate relationship. You shared every emotion and worked together to solve every problem. Remember sharing all your thoughts, emotions, hopes, and dreams? Remember how you wouldn't let anything interfere with this intimacy? Too many times we call these the "good old days."

All Marriages Struggle

If you've chosen to read this chapter today, it may be because your marriage has become difficult. Marriage takes hard work and can be very difficult, but when sin enters, our love for God decreases and our love for each other gets crowded out, lost, or forgotten. God designed marriage to be a blessing, but sometimes it looks more like a bombed out building. Instead of being the total commitment of the total person for the total life, it's just totaled! Marriage, God's intended blessing, becomes difficult and warped. Every married couple learns that *sometimes it's hard to stay married!*

In the last three months several of my dear friends have made known in public what they have felt for months, and, in some cases, years. Their marriages, once vibrant and alive, have died. The final blow to three of them is immorality. The other two "just can't face another day of trying to keep it together." Everyone who loves them has been worried about them. We've all encouraged them, prayed for them, and tried to help. Some have talked when they should have been quiet, and some have been quiet when they should have spoken up. In each of these situations though, there were symptoms—a growing distance between the couple—a growing anger or hurt. A wall of unspoken words and unresolved problems had grown in between man and wife.

Which phase of relationship best describes yours?

When Marriages Die

Unless you begin to take steps to *renew* your relationship, your marriage will become *back-to-back*, more like "married singles," a place where many marriages die. (See chart on the opposite page.)

Sometimes, when a marriage gets sick or dies, everyone feels helpless—just like when someone is physically sick and on life support in a hospital! The patient doesn't seem to know what to do. His friends sit in the waiting room and can only see him for minutes at a time. It's the same way with a sick or dying marriage. We see them fighting for their marriage, and like our friend in the hospital, we wait. We wait for the crisis to pass and the "patient" to get better. Sometimes we wait, only to hear from the doctor that our friend died.

What Makes Us Want to Quit?

The words of a great song say, "Daddy, please find a reason to stay with my mommy. Daddy, we both love you. Please don't leave . . . but if you can't find a reason, Daddy, I really wouldn't mind, if you'd let that reason be me" (Steve and Annie Chapman). I think most unfaithful or divorced folks tried with all their strength to make their marriages work. It wasn't that they couldn't find a reason to stay, but that, when human love ran out, they came to a place where they just couldn't try anymore. Most I know didn't run away; they limped or crawled away just to survive. They had nothing more to give. What was offered wasn't enough. There was nothing left to keep them together. So, what makes us want to quit?

When sin entered the world, it entered all of our lives. It seeps into our relationships. Weariness, unresolved conflicts, unanswered questions and unfinished conversations replace passion and hope. Our dreams are crowded out by responsibilities and the immediate. Our "shared dreams" move in and out of focus and often die. This is one

THE BIRTH AND DEATH OF A MARRIAGE
"When your human love runs out"

FACE TO FACE	SIDE BY SIDE FACE TO FACE	SIDE BY SIDE BACK TO BACK	BACK TO BACK
◆ You are attracted to each other PHYSICALLY.	◆ You share a deepening trust.	◆ You take less time to share with each other	◆ Your marriage becomes more like being married singles
◆ Passionate romance captures your EMOTIONS.	◆ Your friendship grows.	◆ Your responsibilities and assets become burdens	◆ You become more involved with children, friends, jobs, hobbies than each other
◆ Shared dreams focus the MIND.	◆ You combine your energies to see your dreams come true.	◆ There is a growing tension between you	◆ Passionate romance becomes only a memory
◆ Shared promises seal the WILL:	◆ You begin to build a home and family.	◆ Unresolved issues grow like a wall between you	◆ Shared dreams now become individual dreams
"The total commitment of the total person for the total life."	◆ There are increasing times of shared tears, laughter, victories, and defeats.	◆ You focus less on each other and more on children and responsibilities	◆ Promises made now become a prison
	◆ you share a growing intimacy of ◇ mind ◇ will ◇ emotions ◇ body	◆ Sex becomes a duty without intimacy	◆ You have a growing interest in outside relationships
		◆ There is a growing loneliness in each of you	◆ Love and hope dies

The result of sin and selfishness piling up between us

GALATIANS 5:19-21

Selfish ambition, fits of rage, jealousy, hatred, factions, dissensions, drunkenness, lies, idolatry, orgies, envy, immorality, impurity, discord, debauchery, witchcraft

GOD

God's love to us and through us brings healing and restoration

GALATIANS 5:22-26

22But the fruit of the Spirit is love, joy, peace, patience, kindness, goodness, faithfulness, gentleness and self-control. . . . 25Since we live by the Spirit, let us keep in step with the Spirit. 26Let us not become conceited, provoking and envying each other.

of those crisis points in our lives when we have to make critical decisions. In this case, what we choose will either take our marriage through the difficult times or doom it to divorce.

"What Should *I* Do?"

I attended a "Pastors and Wives Conference" where the speakers were a husband and wife who had separated, been restored, and were now serving the Lord together again. The pastor said, "I thank you for asking us to come speak to you, but I am not qualified. Let me introduce you to someone who is." With that he introduced his wife who had trusted the Lord and been used by God to help restore her husband. I remember her words,

> *During the embarrassment and pain of the crisis, one minute I wanted to go beg him to come back. I was feeling guilty for all my failures in the marriage, and so I was willing to accept all the blame and accept him back under any circumstances. The next moment I was focusing on my husband's failures, and I was so hurt and angry I wanted to run away and begin to build a life by myself. What I finally came to was this: I decided to trust the Lord and just be faithful to Him and to my commitments. I didn't want my husband to come back until he was right with God, but if he ever got right with God and wanted to return, he would find me waiting right where he left me.*

One of you may be saying, "But, Bill, I can see what that woman did and how it worked out for her, but what should I do?"

*Should I separate? Stay married, but live apart?

*Should I get a legal separation?

*Should I go see a lawyer and check out my legal options?

*If I don't get a divorce, and continue to see him, will I just be enabling him to "have his cake and eat it too"?

*Should I stay in the house? Should I move to where my family lives?

What should *I* do?

Think You Want Out?

As I write this today I want to ask you two different questions:
"What does *God* want?" (Not: "What do I feel like doing?")

"What *should* you do?" (Not: "What do I want to do?")

If you think you are facing a divorce, whether you are the person who wants out, or the one who is being abandoned, I'm sure you are feeling the conflict of indecision. Maybe you know what you *feel* like doing, or you know what your family or best friends *feel* you should do. Maybe you're "making a list and checking it twice" to figure out how to explain or justify your decision, but what does God want you to do? Make no mistake, God hates divorce! (Mal 2:16). No matter who is at fault, no matter who stays or goes, God hates divorce!

Consider the Consequences

As with broken bodies, broken hearts hurt. No matter who chooses to quit the marriage or whether you feel divorce is your only way out, don't be fooled. Consider the consequences; they're real and lasting.

▶ Divorce hurts. It's never an escape from pain, and it always hurts everyone.

▶ Divorce cuts every heart and mind with wounds that only God can heal.

▶ Divorce will affect you spiritually. You will struggle. It will make you feel, "Somehow I let God down," or, "God let me down." It will affect your prayer life, your worship, your Bible reading, you confidence in your own faith, your freedom to confidently tell people of the God who answers prayer. One woman confided, "Even after being married for 27 years to a wonderful man and father, I still feel pain for my children who were not raised with their biological father."

▶ Divorce bankrupts people financially, emotionally, and physically.

▶ Divorce always changes your friendships. "Our friends" become "his friends" or "her friends," or drift away from both of you! Even "your friends" may become distant, unable to relate to your pain, loneliness, and anger. They may withdraw from you because they don't know what to say or do.

▶ Divorce, for any reason, will change you. No matter how forgiven or forgiving you are, it will leave you hardened, less trusting, more self-protecting and self-centered.

▶ Divorce always leaves holes in the hearts of those divorced, their friends, and their church, but mostly it harms children for a lifetime.

Working through the Trials of Marriage

Years ago I heard someone preach a sermon about Jesus' first miracle. It's been called "When the Wine Runs Out." In John 4 Jesus is visiting a wedding, and there are more guests than refreshment. Jesus' mother, Mary, told the wedding coordinator to go to Jesus and "whatsoever He tells you to do, do it." What a story: the filling of pots with water, Jesus turning them to pots of wine, and the wedding host declaring, "This is the best wine!" Jesus turned a trial into a triumph!

When your wine, or your love, runs out, it may be that you have been giving away your human love, and "it's just run out." Maybe you need the Lord to turn your "water into wine"—your human love into godly, unconditional love. It is limitless.

Seeing Your Mate through God's Eyes

Chances are when you first fell in love you noticed the weaknesses of your mate, and you loved him anyway. Maybe you saw these weaknesses as areas of vulnerability, and you saw an opportunity to protect him. He made you feel needed. Maybe you've come to see these weaknesses more as inconveniences, and you've grown resentful. Maybe your mate had courage enough to believe he might be able to overcome those lifelong flaws because of your love and acceptance. Maybe now, because of your growing resentment, you point out these flaws to him at every opportunity, and he has lost the courage to even try to change.

Have you forgotten? Your mate is a priceless treasure (to God, if not to you). He has an overwhelming value because Jesus Christ died for him! If you, seeing his problems, were to place a price tag on them, equal to the price that you'd pay for them, would you label them "Damaged Goods, Half Off"? Or do you see them through God's eyes and see them as "Priceless!" (Rom 5:8; John 3:16) How have you been treating your mate? As a priceless treasure, one for whom Christ died? As one who belongs to the Lord? You say, "Well, you don't know how stupid he's been! You don't know how he has let me down! You don't know what he said to me! You don't know how he has hurt me!"

And I say, "I thought you loved him, not just enjoyed or used him for what he made you feel or what he did for you." I say, "It sounds like your human love is gone and you need to go to Jesus." What will you find? Real ever-lasting love. God is the real source of love. God is love (1 John 3:1).

Giving God's Love

How do I get it? When we become Christians, the Lord gives us the Holy Spirit who begins to produce the likeness of Jesus in our lives (Gal 5:22). It's God's love *to* us and then God's love *through* us. Please stop and think; maybe you have the wrong definition of love.

I remember a speaker asking me to give the quality of my love a test. He said, "Take 1 Corinthians 13:4 and place your name in the place of 'love.' This will test the quality of love you are giving others."

♦ 1 Corinthians 13:4-8: *Love [Bill] is patient, love [Bill] is kind. It [Bill] does not envy, it [Bill] does not boast, it [Bill] is not proud. It [Bill] is not rude, it [Bill] is not self-seeking, it [Bill] is not easily angered, it [Bill] keeps no record of wrongs. Love [Bill] does not delight in evil but rejoices with the truth. It [Bill] always protects, [Bill] always trusts, [Bill] always hopes, [Bill] always perseveres. Love [Bill] never fails.*

At the speaker's encouragement I gave myself the test and was brought under tremendous conviction. I had been giving away a second-rate love, and I needed to go to the source of love and ask Him to love my wife and children *through* me!

Sometimes Real Love Just Gets Crowded Out!

In Revelation 2:2-5, Jesus identifies how hard the people were working and how they were committed to truth. But they were crowding out love. In verses four and five he says,

⁴But I have this complaint against you. You don't love me or each other as you did at first! ⁵Look how far you have fallen from your first love! Turn back to me again and work as you did at first. If you don't, I will come and remove your lampstand from its place among the churches (NLT).

Have you become so busy doing good things you have quit doing the most important thing? Have you gotten too busy, too distracted, to love the Lord and each other? God has a prescription for lost love. His method for restoring our relationship with Him will also help restore our relationship with our mate. Perhaps this is a project you need to work through.

God's Prescription for Restoring Lost Love

1. Remember

What your love was at first.

Remember . . .

• What first attracted you to him/her. Where you were. What you saw and smelled.

- The first time you touched hands and the first time you kissed.
- The way you felt when you first knew you loved your mate.
- The first intimate touch. The first time you shared sexually.
- A time when you hurt, and your mate comforted you.
- A time when you enjoyed the intimacy, when nothing separated you.

The long term dreams that focused your minds.

Remember . . .

- When you first planned to marry. Who you told first.
- What your first home together was like.
- What your happiest memories were there.
- How you felt when you first heard you were going to have a child.
- The dreams you had for your vocation.
- Your greatest accomplishments together.

The promises you committed yourselves to.

Remember . . .

- "I take you to be my wedded wife/husband. To have and to hold from this day forward; for better for worse, for richer or poorer, in sickness and in health, to love and to cherish, till death do us part, according to God's Holy Word."
- Other promises you made to each other.

2. *Repent.* Repent means: "To have a change of mind that brings about a change in behavior" or "To be sorry enough about your behavior to ask God to help you change."

3. *Redo.* Notice the Scripture doesn't say "re-feel" it says "redo." Do the things you did at first. Feelings come and go. Feeling love comes and goes; choosing to receive love from God so I can give love to my mate is a matter of daily choice.

4. *Or else.* There is always a consequence to our choosing to sin. When we fail to love the Lord, when we fail to love each other, the *lampstand* goes out of our faith, our life, and our relationships. It begins to die.

5. *It's your choice!* You can choose to exhaust yourself by trying to "save your marriage," and no matter what you do, your mate may not cooperate, or you can choose to trust the Lord to live in your life and help you to make right choices that lead to peace of mind even though there may be war in your relationship. What will you choose . . . daily? A path of destruction or a new life?

Practical Projects We Can Try

1. Have you committed yourself to being faithful to God?
2. Have you committed yourself to allowing the Lord to work in and through you?
3. Have you reviewed the promises you made to God and to your mate when you married?
4. Are you (and I hope your mate) being teammates to build a healthy marriage?
5. Are you weeding through your lives, schedule, distractions to focus on what will help you keep from crowding out your relationship with God, your mate, and your children?
6. Are you believing the lie that "quality time" is as good as quantity time? Are you believing time spent in the same room (i.e., watching TV) is as good as time spent listening to each other's heart?
7. Are you allowing the Lord to bring healing in your past so you will be a healthy tool for Him to use in loving your mate? Some of the things that prevent us from investing emotionally in each other are insecurities (past hurts, current behavior—by either spouse, or a belief about who we are and what gives us value), stress (financial, problems with the kids, grief, health, etc.), and unmet expectations (when our mate keeps letting us down, when we don't measure up to our own expectations, or when life just isn't going as planned—extreme debt, gambling addictions, pornography, perfectionism, laziness, alcoholism, molestation of one of the children, physical abuse, deception, dealing with the death of a child, etc.).
8. Do you understand that you and your marriage are *never* a finished product and that *every* person and couple needs to be getting help from someone whose life experience will help you take the next step to maturity?
9. Do you understand that remembering your first love, or learning what God intended your love to be, is only the first step in falling in love again and finding healing for your relationship?
10. All marriages, families, friendships, and church relationships are created and sustained by difficult choices.
11. Are you letting God change and mold your thinking by hiding His word in your heart?

Practical Helps from God's Word

A PRACTICAL BIBLE STUDY ON HOW TO HAVE GOD CHANGE YOU AND YOUR RELATIONSHIPS 1 Peter 2				
WHEN YOU BECOME A CHRISTIAN	2:1 JESUS HELPS YOU BE GENUINE	2:2 JESUS HELPS YOU HUNGER FOR RIGHT THINGS	2:4FF. JESUS HELPS YOU MATURE	2:21 JESUS HELPS YOU BEHAVE
A Christian: Believes in Jesus Belongs to Jesus Is Baptized into Jesus Becomes like Jesus Behaves like Jesus Is never forsaken by Jesus Goes to be with Jesus when he dies	2:1 Get rid of malicious behavior and deceit. 2:1 Don't just pretend to be good. 2:1 Be done with hypocrisy and jealousy.	2:2 Crave pure spiritual milk 2:2 so you can grow up into the fullness of your salvation. 2:2 Cry out as a baby for nourishment.	2:4 Come to Christ who is the cornerstone 2:5 Let God build you as a living stone 2:5 into a spiritual temple, 2:5 into God's holy priest. 2:11 Live as foreigners and aliens here. 2:11 Keep away from evil desires. 2:12 Be careful how you live among unbelieving neighbors. 2:13 Accept all authorities. 2:15 Let good lives silence accusers. 2:15 Respect kings, masters, 3:1 husbands 3:7 wives.	2:21 Expect suffering. 2:21 Follow Jesus' example. 2:22 Don't sin. 2:22 Don't deceive. 2:22 Don't retaliate. 2:23 Don't threaten. 2:23 Leave case in hands of God. 2:23 Be willing to suffer for others' sins. 2:24 Let Him heal your wounds. 2:25 Quit wandering like lost sheep. 2:25 Turn to your Shepherd and Guardian of your soul. 3:1 Wives "in the same way," 3:7 husbands "in the same way," 3:8 all Christians, "all of you," 3:13-18 be ready to give answers for faith.

From my journal December 11, 1971.

It was a hard week. I had decided to divorce my wife, leave my children, and leave the ministry. I had no more energy or hope to run on. A friend of mine asked me as a favor to attend a program on the family, and so as a last resort I attended. The Lord spoke into my life and gave me hope. God was not finished with me yet! If God wasn't finished with me yet, maybe he wasn't finished with my wife. If he wasn't finished with Bobbi or me, maybe he wasn't finished with our marriage or our family. I decided to ask God to forgive me and give me the Love promised in Galatians 5:22.

Concluding Thoughts

I'm so grateful that the Lord and my family showed me true love and were patient with me while true love grew in my heart. When I was first married, I gave a love that frankly wasn't worth giving away. I'm praying that before I'm called to heaven, when all of me and all my old worn-out love is gone, you will see me giving my sweet Bobbi and those in my world only royal love.

I'm praying for you. The Lord wants to fill your life with His love so you can have His love to give to everyone in your world. Thank you for reading this tough chapter.

Dear Family and Friends,

This is a chapter about love.

There are all kinds of definitions of love that after you receive it, still leave you empty. But there's the God kind of love that builds you up and fills the broken places of your heart.

I've seen what love looks like in the Bible when it says in Romans 5:6-8 (NLT), "When we were utterly helpless, Christ came at just the right time and died for us sinners. Now, no one is likely to die for a good person though someone might be willing to die for a person who is especially good. But God showed his great love for us by sending Christ to die for us while we were still sinners."

I've seen what love looks like in my family. Some people called her Lois; we called her Mom or Grandma.

I believe each of our family felt acceptance from my mother. Somehow when we were with her, or even still think of her, we all feel unconditional love. We knew there was nothing we could ever do that would make her stop loving us. Her love was given to us even though we were confused or crazy, successful at our jobs or fired, happy or overburdened. She made us feel believed-in, and she just knew that we would "turn out OK." I don't know how she did it, but she made everyone who knew her feel like he or she was her special favorite. If you want to start a fight at a family reunion, just try convincing other family members that they were not my mom's favorite.

The last day I saw her, Parkinson's and age had stripped her of her strength. She had become a shriveled up little person who struggled to talk. Her thoughts were often unclear, and life had become difficult. But in her presence, I still felt loved. What a gift. That night she went to heaven, but there has never been a day since that I don't think of her and feel closer to God because of her.

She helped me see that when you love and are loved, you will want to keep the rules. I didn't want to disappoint her! When you love and are loved, you want to spend time with each other. When you love and are loved, you never want to say good bye.

As you read this chapter on building a strong love relationship with God and with your mate, I hope you see the love God has for _you_ through Bobbi and me.

Dad/Grandpa/Bill

CHAPTER TWELVE

When You Don't Love Your Mate Anymore

When Love Dies

What happened to "Happily Ever After"? Are you having a hard time loving your husband or your wife? Marriages are intended to be the *total commitment* of the *total persons* for the *total life*. But if that's what it's supposed to be, what happens when love dies?

Two people are drawn together by passionate romance. Their relationship deepens as they share common long-term dreams. There are times, though, when the passion diminishes, the dreams move in and out of focus, and all that holds them together is their commitment to a sacred vow . . . "until death do us part."

One day a woman came into my office and said, "I don't love my husband any more. I'm going to get a divorce." I miserably thought to myself, "Good. Your kind of love isn't worth giving or getting." The problem was, as I listened to her story, I could see myself. I too had a hollow heart. I knew I couldn't give a love to my wife that I simply didn't possess. The love was gone.

How do we, who are created in the image of God, lack the love that it takes to make relationships last? Are we just wounded children who become wounded adults and then go on to create wounded marriages in wounded homes where we raise more wounded children?

How about you?

Maybe you and your spouse are living in the same house, sleeping in the same bed, eating at the same table, sharing the same children, yet, you are each very much alone. Have you longed to be loved all your life? As a child, did you seek love from your parents, only to discover they couldn't give you what they didn't have? Did you seek love from friends, only to find they couldn't understand your desperate need and left? Did you look for love in sex, but only find frustration? Did you search for love in the Bible, but only find truths that made you more miserable? Have you looked for love in the church, but only found other desperate people—all hoping "the right church," the "right doctrine," the "right kind of worship" or the "right kind of preacher" could help soothe the ache in their hearts? Did you search for love in marriage—thinking "at last" you'd found it—but now you find you're still empty?

You Can't Give Away What You Don't Have.
Others Can't Give You What They Don't Already Have.

I could give you a lot of supposition, but, for whatever reason, since my earliest childhood I have been driven to find someone who'd love me. I tested everyone I met with my expectations, but they either couldn't or wouldn't meet my needs—so I drove them away. I could have written the song, "Looking for love in all the wrong places, looking for love in too many faces!"

Then I met Bobbi. She had "bedroom" eyes. (At least, every time I looked in her eyes, I thought of the bedroom.) But when I looked into her heart, I saw her love for the Lord and her desire to serve Him, just as I did. She was so different from anyone I'd ever met; she was the one person I couldn't drive away.

I married her thinking I'd found the love I desperately longed for, but for the next seven years I lived in want, frustration, and doubt. My longing was not for sex, but for an illusive goal I could not clearly define. As I look back, there were only two things wrong with us, but because those two things were wrong, nothing much was right.

What do we really want?

Have you ever wanted something, but you didn't know what it was? Have you ever wanted something, got it, but discovered it wasn't what you wanted after all? I guess that's what happened to me. I knew I wanted to share *real and lasting* love, but I couldn't, because I didn't have it to give away. I didn't even know what it really looked like; I guess I thought one day I'd just find it.

A Love That Lasts

I remember hearing one man say, "If I had shared Jesus with my first wife like I'm sharing Him with my third wife, there wouldn't have been a second wife." It's a cute saying, with a whole lot of truth packed into it. So, what did he mean? What was he really sharing with his present wife? Jesus, the real love that glues two broken people together!

Now Bobbi and I were both devoted Christians. We had Jesus, but there were two obstacles in our way. First, I was married to a Christian who trusted God, but she was married to a man who believed in Jesus, and wanted to serve Him, but didn't know or trust Him. My relationship with Him was based upon truth and a mission, not upon love and a relationship. Second, even after *both* of us knew and trusted the Lord, we didn't share our love for Christ. We were trying to raise a family and serve in the church. We were intimate physically and emotionally, but not spiritually. We did not share Jesus.

After nine years of struggling, we finally went to the Lord, first as individuals, and allowed Him to begin to heal our hearts. As we grew closer to Him, we grew closer to each other. It was after that time that I began to understand, and I wrote to Bobbi:

My Favorite Place

To My Bobbi
It was a place where performance mattered,
A place where passion burned.
Or a place of anger and silence
As backs were often turned.
A Lonely place without touching,
A place of pain and tears;
A place with expectations unmet
Through nights that seemed like years.
But when our human love had vanished,
God gave us real love instead,
And now my favorite place in living
Is with you in our bed.
Our bed is like an island
In a sea of troubled pain;
It's a port in a storm of trials
Or a shelter from the rain.
It's a place of loving and sharing,

Of joy in the middle of tears.
A place where I'm still welcomed
In spite of all my fears.
A place where sex is a blessing,
Where I give and you give to me.
A place where just holding and touching
Is my favorite place to be.
A place that becomes like an altar
Where our deepest prayers are said,
A place where memories are kept alive
With you, in our bed.
A place where I can really be me—
No false smiles or pretend—
A place where I share all my feelings
With you, my cherished, dearest friend.
I love you.
Bill

11/14/95

What changed?

God began to work in my wife, and she found the source of real love. She allowed God to give her real love, and then she brought some to me. Bobbi loved me, even when I didn't know what love was or how to love her in return. She trusted God in her loneliness, and He allowed her to survive all those years, living with a broken unloving husband. Bobbi became my best friend and then became, next to Jesus, the love of my life. What happened?

I'd been preaching about God's love to everyone else, but I finally began to understand what God had been trying to tell me all along. I had been looking for real love for twenty-nine years—seven of which I was married! I was in a frustrating marriage, in a frustrating home, with three frustrating little children . . . and I finally got it! I had been telling others of God's love and grace, but I hadn't been accepting it for myself.

God is love. He is the source of real love and He loves even me! He loves me just as I am, just where I am—He loves me! I finally understood that if I'd been the only sinner on earth, He would still have loved me and sent me Jesus to be my Savior! Jesus still would have gone to the cross and a grave for me! And He promised to do a good work in me. Think of it—God wasn't finished with me. There was hope! God would place His Holy Spirit into my life and He would produce a royal kind of love that I could give away! I could now begin to give real love because God had given it to me!

It's amazing how that little glimmer of hope helped me. Next I thought, "If God isn't finished with me, maybe He isn't finished with Bobbi!" I decided there was hope yet for my marriage. I looked at the children and thought, "Maybe He isn't finished with the kids yet either! Maybe there is hope and help for our broken home!" And I was right.

Love Restored

As that year progressed, I felt God's love move through me. I was able to give real love! He helped me see my family through His eyes and to have true love for them. **He was real love** and we shared Him with each other!

I remember the morning true love came to our bed.

I woke up, rolled over, and looked at Bobbi to discover that after seven years of frustration and two years of receiving God's love to give to her, *I had fallen in love with my wife!* We still had all the open wounds and scars my lack of love had produced. We still had the dysfunctional home and the tremendous debt. We still didn't know how to be healthy people, marriage partners, or parents, but I had found what I had spent my life looking for, I had found real and lasting love.

Where are we now, 42 years later? We are still learning, still growing in the right direction, but we have by no means "arrived." Sometimes changes in health, medication, and the number of our birthdays have affected our passionate romance. Sometimes our shared dreams move in and out of focus. Sometimes it's our commitment to be faithful "until death do us part" that causes us to hold on, but then, after a few tough days together, we remember the source of the love that's been our glue for 41 years isn't in our own efforts. It's in Christ. It's given to us and through us from the Lord. Then that romance is rekindled, the dreams move into focus, and the intimacy of sharing all we are, body, mind, will, and emotions, is held together like glue through God's love to us. Bobbi has become my best friend, my partner, the one who shares true intimacy with me. It's not "me"; it's not "her." It's "us"—a relationship of three, as the Lord holds us together (Eccl. 4:9).

As we grow old together, and we're not "old" yet, I know that God will continue His work in us—as individuals and as a couple! I believe our best years are those to come because it only gets better as we grow closer to the Lord. Still I wonder, will we become just good friends who live in the same house and sleep in the same bed? Will we continue to fall in love with each other over and over again?

What will our old age bring? If we are at some point placed in a nursing home, I hope you accidentally "catch" us lying in the same bed, arms around each other remembering the passion of our youth, smiling, and reliving the dreams that we have shared together. I hope you see two people who have found a quality of intimacy where their hearts beat as one and who continue to grow together in their love for the Lord, joyfully clinging to their commitment to God and each other.

God is love, real love. He is the glue! I have come to the place where I now trust and know that *"there is one thing right with me, and because of that one thing, all the things that are broken in me can be healed!"* Philippians 4:13 says it this way, *"I can do all things through Christ!"*

Commit Today

*We believe God's desire for marriage is the **total commitment** of the **total person** for the **total life**.*

We understand that marriage is an intensely intimate relationship between two persons in which passionate romance captures the affections, a long-term dream focuses the mind, and a sacred vow seals the will.

We know that our marriage will not be without changing circumstances and periodic crisis. Our dreams will move in and out of focus, and there will come times when only our commitment, "till death do us part" will hold our marriage together.

We trust God to restore our love in times of difficulty.

We commit ourselves to focusing on our Heavenly Father so we may keep our commitments—knowing that romance will be rekindled and the dream renewed.

Source Unknown

Consider This Project to Get Your Marriage Back in Focus

It is intended to help you see beyond the present problems and to help you remember the early days of your marriage.

Project One:

Read the above statements out loud. Working together, paraphrase them into your own words. Listen to each other. Make sure that both of you agree on these statements about marriage. Make this commitment together.

Project Two

Interview five couples of your own choosing. Tell them, "We are doing a project to strengthen our marriage. Can we ask you two questions about your marriage?" If they agree, ask them: "If you were able to start your marriage over again, what would you do the same? What would you do differently?" (It's important to take notes and spend time together discussing their answers.)

Project Three

Plan your next two dates: Flip a coin; whoever wins plans the first date. The other person plans the second date. The "date planner" must ask, "What would please my mate?" On these dates, plan to identify and discuss the *long-term* dreams that brought you together. Before your date, each of you, individually, should spend time with God asking Him to help you establish the promises *you* are willing to make to God and to each other, and asking Him to be the power to keep the promises and the glue to keep you together.

Dear Family and Friends,

It's amazing how learning you are going to be a dad changes your thinking and focus.

When Jim and then Melissa were born, I still thought I knew what to do as a parent. I remember thinking, "Now it's my turn. I'm going to do better than my dad," but I didn't.

When Joni was born I thought, "I can see I'm doing some things better than my dad, but I am starting to fail."

When Angela was born I thought, "Four of them? I'm overwhelmed with three! How did my dad do as well as he did?"

When Melody was born, the fifth child in six-and-one-half years, I thought, "How can this be happening? I'm failing as a person, a husband, and as a father, and now there are five? No wonder my dad shut down emotionally and started to withdraw!"

I regret the years I looked at my physical father and tried to be a better parent than he was. In fact, the older I am, the more I'm like him. I look in the mirror and see him; when I face difficult times I have the same depression he faced; I face the same kinds of health issues he faced.

As I look back on my whole parenting experience, I realize I had my eyes on the wrong dad. I'm not supposed to do better, or as well as my physical dad. I need to get my eyes on my Heavenly Dad and act like Him.

Dad/Grandpa/Bill

CHAPTER THIRTEEN

When You Fail as a Parent

If You Give Yourself the Wrong Job Description as a Parent, It Will Break Your Heart!

One of my children said the other day, "Dad, I don't know what to do with my teenager." In that moment I was flooded with my own memories of how I had let him down when he was that age, and all I could say was, "I don't know what to tell you." Later that day I e-mailed him and said, "I've been praying for you, and I do know what to suggest to you. You are a much better parent than I was, and your son is a better kid than you were. Just keep doing what you are doing. If your grandma were here, she would probably say to you what she said many times to me. 'He will be all right. He has a good heart.'"

What can you do when your babies turn into teenagers? Have they grown into adult bodies but still act like children? Maybe they used to want to spend time with you and do what you thought was best, but now they don't want you around, don't listen, and question everything you say.

Maybe you're wondering what you did wrong. Maybe you've found yourself, more than once, lying awake at night, doubting yourself. "Am I being a good enough parent? Do my children see Christ in me? Am I demonstrating a faith they'll want for themselves? Do they really know the Lord, or do they just know about Him?"

Watch Out for the Trap!

If you are not careful, you will find yourself trapped into the false belief that if *you* are a good enough parent, *you* will be able to save your children. If you try harder, read more, are more consistent, your children will certainly become Christians. Maybe you've read and claimed Proverbs 22:6 for yourself: *"Train up a child in the way he should go, even when he is old he will not depart from it"* (NASB).

When you look at your family and the families around you, are you confused? I sure was. I was puzzled because I saw others who hadn't raised their children in church, or who hadn't tried half as hard as I had to be a good parent, and produced great children. Yet I was *really* struggling with my children. I couldn't figure it out. What was wrong? Had God misled me and not kept His promise?

I know a dear minister's wife who raised her children in a Christian home, but her oldest child, who is sixty-seven-years old, is still not saved. She said to me, "Well, I still have hope. You know what the Scripture says, 'Raise up a child in the way he should go, and when he is old he will not depart from it.'" There it is again, like a "guarantee." Or is it? Shouldn't she be able to find comfort in knowing that since she raised him in a Christian home and in a church, he will absolutely become a Christian? Does the Scripture really promise that if we raise them properly, in spite of their free will and our parenting imperfections, our children really have no choice but to come back to those teachings when they are old? *"If we do, they absolutely will"*? If we don't look closer, we can fall into a heartbreaking trap.

A Closer Look at God's Promise

If I really want to "claim this promise," I have to keep the commands . . . perfectly. So let's look at what "raise up a child in the way he should go" really means.

♦ Deuteronomy 6:4-9: *⁴The LORD our God, the LORD is one. ⁵Love the LORD your God with all your heart and with all your soul and with all your strength. ⁶These commandments that I give you today are to be upon your hearts. ⁷Impress them on your children. Talk about them when you sit at home and when you walk along the road, when you lie down and when you get up. ⁸Tie them as symbols on your hands and bind them on your foreheads. ⁹Write them on the door frames of your houses and on your gates.*

Look at the context of these commands. Beginning in Deuteronomy 6:2, I am instructed:

- to observe, obey, and keep these commands,
- to keep them upon my heart, not just on my walls or in my mouth,
- to let no person or thing take God's place because there is no other god,

- to love God with all my heart, soul, and strength,
- to impress God's commands on my children, teaching them when:
  - we sit at home
  - we walk along the road
  - we go to sleep and when we wake up
- to wear His teachings on my hands and forehead and place them on the walls of my home.

If I keep the commands, I can claim the promises.

Reality Check

How are you doing at "keeping the commands" so you can "claim the promises"? Maybe you're thinking, "I've loved the Lord, with most of my heart, soul, and strength. I've taught my children . . . a lot!" Maybe you've tried really hard, have kept most of these commands, most of the time. Or maybe you have to confess, "I haven't kept the commands at all. Is there any hope for me?"

I must have tried a thousand different methods of being a good parent and a "priest and shepherd" to my own family—and for a thousand different reasons, I failed. I never got up even *one* morning and thought, "I think I'll be a lousy dad today," but often I was. The reality was, I did *some* of His commands, *some* of the time. As close as I came to following these commands, close isn't good enough. I failed.

I don't want God to bless me on how well I've kept the commands. I want forgiveness and help from God. I want Him to fill in the gaps in my parenting and save my children! I need His grace!

God's Grace

I remember going to the doctor because I was sick (more sick of heart than of body). My hopes for being a good parent were crushed. Rebellion and conflict filled my home. As I sat in the doctor's office, I picked up an old *Reader's Digest* and read the story of a woman who wrote,

> Lord, when I wake up in the night, and I don't know where my child is or what he is doing, please help me remember that you love my child even more than I do.

There in the waiting room of the doctor's office I found the promise I needed! I have to confess I stole that page right out of that book and carried it with me for years!

I want you to remember this: If all my children are Christians today, it's *not* because they had parents who were good enough or faithful enough. It's not because we found a magic verse in Scripture, and we certainly didn't do everything right. No, they are Christians today *in spite of us* and *because of a faithful God* who loves them and never gave up on them.

The Truth

If your children could become Christians *by your parenting*, they wouldn't need Jesus to be their savior. That doesn't mean parents get to quit trying; the primary tools God uses are parents!

The test of your life and home will not be whether your children become Christians, but rather, if you loved, trusted, and obeyed the Lord yourself. The test of your children's lives will be whether they listened to the truth and chose to love and obey the Lord themselves.

The children were never ours; they are on loan from the Lord. They are *first* His children. It was never "just up to us" to raise them. God uses parents, extended families, churches, friends, schools, policemen, and governments to raise children to maturity.

The bottom line is, when everything else fails, including we parents, God still loves our children . . . more than we do! We cannot follow the commands perfectly, but His grace is perfect.

A Parent's Job Description

So, if my job isn't to raise Christian children, what is my job description?

One—*My job description includes becoming what God designed me to be and running the race he has set before me.*

I am to:

- → Believe on
- → Belong to
- → Become like
- → Behave like
- → Bring people to
- → Be forever with

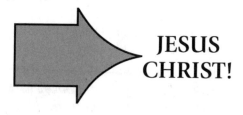

JESUS CHRIST!

Two—*My job description is to partner with God in his mission to lead my children to Christ.*

If your child hears from you about Christ but doesn't see Christ in your life, he or she won't want the kind of Christianity you are trying to give. If your child knows *about* Jesus Christ, but *doesn't know Him* as savior, the child will first reject Jesus, then you, and finally the other authorities in his life.

If your child doesn't know Jesus Christ as Lord and Savior, there is really only one thing wrong with him. But because that one thing is wrong with him, not much will be right with him.

> The goal of our parenting is to partner with God in raising children who will spend eternity with us in heaven. as we raise them in the Lord, they will grow from children to become people who **believe** in, **belong** to, **become** like, **behave** like, and **bring people to Jesus.** This is accomplished according to *2 Timothy 3:10-17* by our:
>
> **modeling   protecting   instructing   disciplining   releasing**

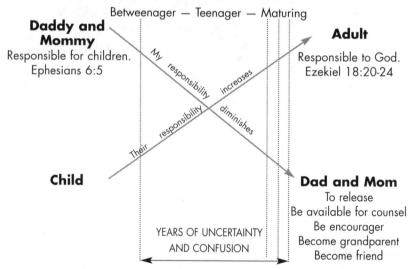

Role	Changing Responsibilites	Role

Betweenager — Teenager — Maturing

Daddy and Mommy
Responsible for children.
Ephesians 6:5

My responsibility increases
Their responsibility diminishes

Adult
Responsible to God.
Ezekiel 18:20-24

Child

Dad and Mom
To release
Be available for counsel
Be encourager
Become grandparent
Become friend

YEARS OF UNCERTAINTY
AND CONFUSION

> Creating a relational environment
> where biblical leadership takes place

Three—*My job description includes submitting to God's leadership in my life and home.*

Unless God builds my life and family, they will fail.

♦ Psalm 127:1-5 (NASB): ¹*Unless the LORD builds the house, they labor in vain who build it. Unless the LORD guards the city [home, church, nation], the watchman keeps* *awake in vain. ²It is vain for you to rise up early, to retire late, to eat the bread of painful labors, for He gives to His beloved even in his sleep. ³Behold, children [godly children] are a gift from the LORD; the fruit of the womb is a reward. ⁴Like arrows in the hand of a warrior [parent] are the children of one's youth. ⁵How blessed is the man whose quiver is full of them; they shall not be ashamed when they speak to their enemies in the gates.*

Without God working in and through us, our children may be more like well-sharpened knives that intentionally hurt us than like "arrows in a quiver." We must let God lead: through the truths and wisdom revealed in the Scriptures, through the prompting of the Holy Spirit, through the help of godly wise counsel, and through constant prayer. We may be able to "build the house," but only God can "build the home."

Four—*My job description includes being responsible to God for my children for a limited time.*

As you read Hebrews 12:10 you will discover that God gives parents responsibility for their children for a "little while." *"For our earthly fathers disciplined us for a few years, doing the best they knew how. But God's discipline is always right and good for us because it means we will share in his holiness"* (NLT).

It's been hard for me to identify the limitations of my role as a parent. It's also been difficult to step back and turn the responsibility for converting my children, for disciplining them, for no longer being the "answer man," the one who rescues them from their problems, to God. When they are young, God uses parents as the primary tool in their lives, but as they grow, our role changes from primary tool, to support tool. God takes over and finishes the job in their lives.

▌ At what age is the responsibility of disciplining our children ended? Is it as long as they will let us be a tool in their lives? Is it as long as they live in our homes? Is it until they reach the legal age according to the law? I observe that when the people of Israel failed to trust God and enter into the Promised Land, God judged those who were 20 and older, but did not punish the children 0-19 for their parents' decisions (Num 14:18).

▌ Does God hold me responsible for my grown children, or am I responsible as a child for my parents decisions? I've found comfort in the Lord's instructions through Ezekiel to His people. See Ezekiel 18:1-32.

  ▌ 18:4-5—All of us belong to the Lord. It's not my child, my family, my total responsibility.

  ▌ 18:10-13—A good man can have bad sons.

▌18:14-18—A bad man can have good sons.

▌18:21—God offers to restore any repentant rebel.

▌18:21-23—God's will is restoration, but he gives every person the choice.

▌18:24-26—A righteous man can become a rebel from God and be judged.

▌18:27-28—A wicked man can turn away from his wicked ways and live.

▌18:29-30—God will judge us as individuals according to our life and deeds.

▌18:32—God takes no pleasure in judging sinners.

Five—*My job description includes doing the best I know how* (Heb 12:10). This doesn't mean I can remain ignorant of my responsibilities. I have been given God's Word to instruct me. There are lots of godly parenting resources written by Christian parents who are older and wiser.

Sometimes We Have to "Begin Again . . . and Again . . . and Again"

I remember when Bobbi and I recognized that our different views of parenting were allowing the children to "divide and conquer."

▲ We took a few days away together to catch our breath and make a plan.

▲ Bobbi and I determined we would be partners with God and each other in seeing our home become what God wanted it to be.

▲ We determined to read together everything the Bible has to say about parenting and let the Lord be the one who set the boundaries for our parenting.

▲ Bobbi began reading books about parenting to me, and we discussed our way through their advice.

▲ We made a list of the people we knew who were being successful parents, and we determined to ask them, "If you were able to start over as parents, 1) what would you do the same, and 2) what would you do differently?"

▲ We determined to ask the Lord to help us identify the areas where we had failed and establish a new direction for our parenting.

▲ We called a family meeting, and through tears and repentance we asked their forgiveness for the areas where we had failed.

▲ We began to teach them what we were learning about what God wanted for our home.

When something is broken, love and forgiveness give second chances, but only true repentance and disciplined changes in the parents will ultimately bring about real changes in the whole family.

What do we do when we look at our children and we see the coming pressures and tests they will have to endure? It was about that time I discovered Song of Solomon 8:8-10.

> ⁸We have a little sister, and she has no breasts; What shall we do for our sister on the day when she is spoken for? ⁹If she is a wall, we shall build on her a battlement of silver; but if she is a door, we shall barricade her with planks of cedar. ¹⁰I was a wall, and my breasts were like towers; then I became in his eyes as one who finds peace (NASB).

What do you do when you look at your daughter, sister, granddaughter, or friend and you see her maturing into a young woman?

What can you, as the responsible adult, do to help her be prepared to face the pressures of life, sexuality, peer pressure?

What should you do for her if she is able to face the pressures and temptations successfully?

What should you do if she is easily swayed by the words and pressures that surround her?

As I look back at my own parenting experience, I too often failed to act until there was a crisis, and then I reacted. Looking back, I wish I had used this passage as a pattern for my own actions.

1. **Plan ahead, be prepared.** Look at the present and future needs and pressures your children face. What shall we do when (fill in the blank)? You could have a date with your mate and role-play the many possibilities your child will face. You would ask yourself, "What would the Lord want us to do or say in certain situations?"

2. **Don't overreact if one of your children fails.** When one of the children failed, I overreacted and our daughter Joni wrote to me,

   "Dad, I know you are trying harder to be a better father, but sometimes it's really difficult to understand. I'm trying to be the best I can because I feel that if I make one mistake, everything you have worked for will go down the drain. But I don't think the girls and I can go through the rest of our years at home feeling that you don't trust us."

   What should we do for children who choose to do right? Solomon wrote, "*If they are a wall, we shall build battlements of silver on her."* I understand this to mean that if they face the pressure or temptations like a wall, standing firm, not easily influenced, we should put them on display. Trust them, give them earned privileges.

3. What should we do for children who make poor choices? Solomon wrote, *"If they are a door (easily opened), we shall barricade her with planks of cedar."* **When a child fails, love and forgiveness is to be given, but trust is to be earned.** Immature children need protection, rules, limitations. If they fail, place "planks of cedar" fences around them so they can mature.

4. **Look forward to the day they mature and the fences can be lowered and finally removed.** I remember when one of my children was going off to college in California. She said, "Daddy, you are worried about me, aren't you?" I said, "Yes, there are so many pressures from being so far from home." She reached out and hugged me and said, "It's okay, Dad. I'm a wall."

I'm so grateful that God has given me and all of you a chance to grow from infants through the teenage years where we needed fences to protect us and help us mature to the place where we can be strong walls. I'm proud of what God is doing in us, and I can see Him working in each of my grandchildren.

What do you do when you see rebellion in your small children? Let God's Word establish the rules for the home, and ask Him to help you keep the rules yourself and help you discipline the children. Be humble enough to seek counseling for yourself and for your family. Be willing to have the Lord send other people, family, friends, church leaders into the life of your child to help. If you see rebellion in the heart of your school age children begin to place fences around them and be willing to make the fences higher or lower depending on their behavior.

What do you do if the fences don't work and the teen keeps "jumping the fence"? Be willing to give appropriate punishment. Maybe you need to restrict their out-of-the-home contacts for a time. Or, think of this: a teenager wants to be left alone in his room. It's there he can talk to his friends on the phone in private. It's there he can get lost in his music or games or TV. What if you put up the fence of removing all privileges other than a mattress to sleep on and minimal food to eat? James Dobson's son says, you don't want to endure the Dobson Grounding. He has spoken of his parents removing *everything* from his room except his mattress.

What do you do if your child jumps the "fence" of your home and no longer is willing to let God establish what is right and wrong, and refuses the discipline of your home? The Bible gives us instructions for dealing with immorality, worshiping other gods, homosexuality, stealing, drunkards or drug users, or swindlers (1 Cor 6:9-10; 5:9-11).

No matter the condition of the relationships in your home, God can make it different!

Remember, it's not *your* home, *your* family. Remember it's not all *your* responsibility.

Remember, God loves your family more than you do, and He wants to help get your family back on track.

I'm glad the Lord is helping me learn to be a better dad than I was a daddy. Please remember, our lives, marriages, and homes will never be perfect till heaven.

Preparation for the Race	Guidelines for the Race	Disciplines for the Race!
Hebrews 11:6	**Hebrews 12:1-12**	**Hebrews 12:10–13:6**
Hebrews 11:16	**12:1**–Run, not walk	**12:10**–"Our parents disciplined for a few years as doing the best they knew how"
Hebrews 12:1	**12:1**–Run with endurance (to finish the race)	**12:10**–"God's discipline is always right"
12:1–Hope–Others have finished the race; so can we!		**12:12**–"Take a grip"
	12:1–Run the race set in front of us	**12:12**–"Stand firm"
		12:13–"Mark out your path ahead," Psalm 71
	12:1–Run with your eyes on Jesus and His example	**12:13**–"Live so those who follow you will become strong," Ps 119:67, 105-112
12:1–Strip off that which slows us down	**12:2**–Run with your faith in Jesus	**12:14**–"Try to live in peace with everyone"
	12:3–Run and don't give up	**12:14**–Try to live a holy life and be a witness to the unsaved
12:1–Strip off the sin that hinders our progress	**12:4**–Run and don't forget God's instructions	**12:15**–"Look out for each other" See also Heb 10:25.
	12:5–Run expecting God's discipline	**12:15**–Watch out to eliminate any unbelief because it will corrupt everyone
12:1–Enter the race!	**12:10-11**–Run expecting discipline to produce His holiness and a harvest of right living	**13:1**–"Continue to love each other"
		13:2-3–Show hospitality to others and don't forget those in prison for their faith
		13:4–Remain faithful in your marriage
		13:5-6–Remember, "God is faithful"

Romans 8:28-29 (NLT)

And we know that God causes everything to work together for the good of those who love God and are called according to his purpose for them. For God knew his people in advance, and he chose them to become like his Son.

Something to Think About from Hebrews 11:1–13:6

1. Are you believing in and trusting God to help you in your life and family?
    ➤ What questions do you have that need answers?
    ➤ Where will you look to find the answers?
2. Since you cannot teach what you do not know and you cannot lead where you will not go . . .
    ➤ Do you have God's goal for *your* life? (Heb 11:6,16)
    ➤ How do you define "winning" "For me to live is _____."
3. Discuss how life, marriage, and family are like a race.
    ➤ What things would you have to strip off or change in your life to bring pleasure to God?
    ➤ As you read Hebrews 12:1-11, please discuss or describe the racecourse that God has set before you (problems, difficulties, challenges).
    ➤ As you read Hebrews 12:10–13:6, consider the practical instructions given to help you finish your race, fulfill your assignment, and keep your eyes on Jesus.

Dear Family and Friends,

Parenting—nothing has given me greater joy or greater pain.

If you could go back in time with me, you would see many times when one of our children was rebelling from God and us. All Bobbi and I could do was huddle together in our bed.

We had tried individually to fix our family, but failed. Sometimes Bobbi would try and I wouldn't be able to. Sometimes I would try and she just couldn't try again. Sometimes we would try together and find solace in the fact that, even though our rebel was still running, we weren't alone. We had come to the end of us, and so we lay there together and let God hold us together.

- Ecclesiastes 4:9-12: [9]Two people can accomplish more than twice as much as one; they get a better return for their labor. [10]If one person falls, the other can reach out and help. But people who are alone when they fall are in real trouble. [11]And on a cold night, two under the same blanket can gain warmth from each other. But how can one be warm alone? [12]A person standing alone can be attacked and defeated, but two can stand back to back and conquer.

In our marriage and parenting there have been times when two (Bobbi and I) was not enough. Our old efforts at creating a family had failed. All we could do was run to the Lord and ask Him to hold us together and help us _rebuild a home to come home to!_

- Ecclesiastes 4:12: "Three are even better, for a triple-braided cord is not easily broken."

We have discovered that when our cord of two is frayed and breaking, the Lord becomes our third cord that held onto us when we didn't have the strength to hold onto each other or to our children.

We have discovered that when we are afraid, God is faithful. When we don't have any answers, or know what to say, He is faithful. When we didn't know where our rebel was or what he or she was doing, God was—and is and will be—faithful!

In those moments, we just held onto each other. God became the third strand in our braided cord, and He held on to us.

Thanks for reading,
Dad/Grandpa/Bill

CHAPTER FOURTEEN

When Your Children Are Driving You Crazy

A Chapter for Parents of Preteens, Teens, and Children in Adult Bodies!

Quick Answers to Parenting Are Easy When It's Not Your Own Child.

Have you noticed that most "How-To" books on parenting are written by people before they have children? If you survive the uncertainty of being the parent of preteens, teens, and children in adult bodies, you will have fewer answers and more testimonies. You'll learn that the "How-To" strategies didn't work, but you will discover, God is faithful. What do I mean? When the children are small it's easy to quote Scripture and make pronouncements of "you are not going to act like that in this family." As the children gr0w, what you assume will work won't.

With some of the children, being a parent was easy. With others, it was difficult, but what do you do when it seems nothing is working?

It's easy to "make a plan," "establish the rules," "demand that they obey," but what should we do when what we believe should work doesn't, and what we say isn't listened to?

Through my years of counseling other parents, I've found that quick answers are easy when it's not my own child. If it's *your* child, I can step back emotionally and see the problem and possible solutions. When it's *my* kid . . . well, let me illustrate.

In the middle of our crazy-broken-family period of parenting, one of our children was in rebellion, one was pregnant, one had withdrawn from our family for reasons I didn't understand, we were in financial ruin, and I was facing a nervous collapse. I couldn't get our rebel to go to counseling, so I decided I would go. The counselor asked me to tell him our situation, and when it came to our rebel, he said, "What would you tell other parents if the rebel was acting like this in their home?" I thought for a moment and said, "I'd probably say, 'Throw the bum out.'" He said, "Throw the bum out." I sat quietly for a moment and said, "I can't; he's *my* bum."

When it's your own "rebel," somehow it's different. The devil, some of your friends, and even you, become "accusers," reminding you of all the things you did wrong as a parent. You remember words you wish you hadn't said and all the things you could have done differently. Talk about times of trials and troubles!

The Problem with a Testimony: It Requires a Test.

The Crisis in Your Home Brings an Opportunity for Each Family Member to Face His Need for Christ

Welcome to reality. Trials and trouble *will* come. There will come times when our children will stop walking on our feet and start walking on our hearts. When this time comes, our own faith will be tested, and they will discover they need a faith in God of their own. I believe there are several reasons for this: 1) We can't please God without a faith of our own (Heb 11:6), 2) because God loves each of us (Hebrews 12), and 3) because borrowing someone else's faith just won't work. Each of us must come to a point of decision—to make faith in God our own. Often it isn't easy.

Each of us will encounter circumstances and face choices when others can't help us. We face enemies others can't protect us from. Perhaps it will be the consequences of poor decisions that will drive us as individuals from *knowing about* God to *believing in and trusting* God. If you want your own faith, or the faith of your children, to become full of faith instead of just facts and to become dynamic Christians instead of "dead" church members, each of us will have to face suffering. Only when we discover our own need for a savior will we fall at the feet of Jesus and fully accept His grace offering. Bobbi would say that her entire parenting changed when she could lift each of our children up to the Lord and say, "Whatever it takes Lord, I want them to be saved."

It's Vital to Know Whether the One You Love Is "Lost" or Has Chosen to Run Away.

It seems like everyone gets lost sometimes. At times we are like the lost sheep in Luke 15:1-3. We wander away in the wilderness and need to be found. Sometimes we are like the lost coin in Luke 15:7-9. We feel misplaced in our own homes! We need someone to search for us, find us, and rejoice that we are found. Sometimes we get lost on purpose. In Luke 15:11-32 we read of the selfish choices the lost (prodigal) son made.

Our children loved Jesus when they were young, and then one by one, we watched each of them test their "borrowed faith." All the doubts and questions of life frightened them. Some, like sheep, got lost. Some, like the prodigal, used those doubts and fears as an excuse for following their own selfish natures. As a parent, I've come to understand a kid's childishness, weakness, and even failure as part of growing and learning, but outright rebellion hurts everybody. When sin enters a life, a marriage, or a family, the result is separation from God, from others, and from themselves. Still, I know that trust in God is developed through difficulties.

Do you see signs of rebellion in your home?

Recognizing the Road to Rebellion

Let's look closer at Luke 15:11-32, as Jesus illustrates the downward spiral of the prodigal:

1. He became **dissatisfied** with his present life. You might see this when your child constantly gripes and complains.

2. He became **demanding**. The prodigal told his father, *"Give me."* You may notice similar signs in your son or daughter. His whole world will be all about himself. I- me- my- mine!

3. He chose to **depart**. The Bible tells us, *"He gathered everything together and left."* Your child will take everything she thinks is hers, and along with those things, she will take your hopes for a loving relationship with her and say, "I don't need you! I can do better on my own!"

4. He wasted his time and treasure in a life of **debauchery**. We read in Scripture that he squandered his estate with loose living—living like an animal rather than one created in the image of God. Your child's choices will put his health and future at risk, and he will squander all your hope for him or all you gave him in a reckless lifestyle.

5. When his money and influence was gone, he became **destitute**. *"No one was giving anything to him."* His choices will use him up,

and when there is nothing left for his so-called friends to take from him, they will leave him for new people to take advantage of.

6. He will become **distressed**, upset, overwhelmed. Ultimately, your son or daughter will become like a sheep without a shepherd (Matt 9:36).

There are some more "Ds" I can think of: downcast, spiritually dead, deluded, dominated, damaged, drunk, drugged, divorced, despairing, doubting, deranged, dropped-out, disinterested, diseased, dysfunctional, and destructive.

Do you remember the hopes you had for your children when they were born? Can you remember when they were open-faced and you could see their hearts? Do you remember when they started withdrawing from you? From good friends to chase after bad? When they started rejecting your counsel? When they started walking away from God?

Is there any hope for the prodigal to be restored?

Like the prodigal in Jesus' illustration, the story doesn't have to end there. Jesus came to set us free from our lives of sin and destruction. God offers a way out! He waits, like the father in the story, for His prodigal to return.

Hope along the Road to Restoration

Let's continue our study of Luke 15: 11-32 as it illustrates the prodigal's trip home:

1. He **realized** his situation. *"When he came to his senses . . ."*

2. He decided to **repent**, becoming willing to tell his father, *"I have sinned against heaven and in your sight. . . . I am no longer worthy to be called your son."*

3. He knew he must **return** to his father. *"I will get up and go to my father."* A changed heart produces changed behavior, not just regret. Before our prodigal can get right with his earthly father, he needs to get right with his Heavenly Father.

4. In brokenness and humility he started toward home, allowing the father to **restore** him to himself. **"But while he was still a long way off, his father saw him, and felt compassion for him, and ran and embraced him and kissed him."**

5. He **received** the forgiveness of his father. When the prodigal returned home, his father declared, *"He was dead and has come to life again; he was lost and has been found."* And they *"began to be merry."*

6. The prodigal still had to make **restitution** for his choices. He had to face the consequences of his sin. Every one of us can choose to sin, and "our father" may forgive us, but every sin has its consequences.

I've often wondered how the story ends. I know the prodigal son was restored to his father, but what was "the rest of the story"? In the Scripture the father says to the older son, *"All that is mine is yours."* In my life there are always people around me who don't understand when the Lord forgives me or takes me back. They are angry when God gives me what I need instead of what I deserve. They focus on reminding me of my past rather than praising God for the changes He is making in my present.

I think of the sin and subsequent consequences of his forgiven sins. I think of those who constantly reminded the Apostle Paul of his forgiven past.

My Prayer:

> "Lord when I'm reminded of my past failure, please remind me of Your great forgiveness. When I see the wonderful changes You are making in those around me, please help me be a good 'forgetter' of their past and join You in cheering them on in their present."

Seek the Lost!

No matter the reason for becoming lost, *Jesus wants us found!* In Luke 15:1-3, Jesus is criticized for spending time with lost people. The superreligious people of His day would rather Jesus had hated the sinners or simply ignored them. They might have tolerated Jesus welcoming the sinners when *they* came to *Him*, but the religious leaders couldn't stand it when *Jesus sought out* the lost and rejoiced when they "were found."

Do you have a lost sheep in your home? Go find them! (Ezek 34:1-10) Is there someone lost, ignored, forgotten, in your own home—like the coin? Don't give up until you have searched for him and found him. Is there a rebel growing up in your home, or one who has run from your home? Try to understand that rebellion is first of all against

God and then you! There is one thing wrong with the rebel: he is wrong with God. But because of that one thing, he is separated from God and now everyone in his world.

Leading the Lost Home

Before you can lead the lost home, you have to know "where they are" and how they got there. As we saw in the story of the prodigal son, the road to rebellion is a progression of downward choices. In Romans 1:18-32 the Apostle Paul further explains this spiraling process. First the rebel suppresses the truth, then he rejects God, and, becoming wise in his own eyes, finally makes a god of his own. Having rejected the living God and His laws, he joins the army of people who are against God.

Leading the lost home is a process that includes careful observation, prayer, and often big adjustments on your part. Remember that things often get worse before they get better.

A PRODIGAL SON'S DOWNWARD SLIDE TO JUDGMENT	
Luke 15:11-32	**Resulting in:**
1. 15:11-12–Knew father but rejected him and values.	1. Dissatisfied, unhappy, ungrateful, demanding.
2. 15:12-13–Considered his father dead, he demanded his inheritance.	2. He separated himself from his father and left home.
3. 15:13–He wasted his life and inheritance.	3. His money and friends ran out.
4. 15:14-16–His life and dreams were ruined.	4. He was starving and alone.
5. 15:25-32–He destroyed all his relationships.	5. His brother hated him.

TRACK YOUR PRODIGAL CHILD'S LIFE TO THIS POINT	
The Downward Spiral	**The Upward Climb**
1. Dissatisfaction	5. Reality Living with the consequences
2. Departure	4. Restored
3. Dissipation	3. Returned
4. Destitute	2. Repent
5. Distressed	1. Realize

A Parent Project

1. Take a close look at your home. Ask God to help you discover what each of your children truly needs. Has a child become a lost sheep? Do you see him acting childish? Immature? Is he rushing into decisions because he is not thinking through the issues? Do you need to take more time with her? Sharing her interests? Hobbies? Getting to know her friends? Are you listening to his concerns and helping him help those he is concerned about? Are you helping her find out who she is so she will know where she fits? Are you valuing what God has already done in her life, or are you just being critical of what God has yet to do? Act like Jesus and leave what you are doing and go find him! Go back and review the material on the parent's job description and make sure you are partnering with God in His plans for your children's lives. Go find them!

2. Has your home become filled with so much conflict or crisis that your child has become lost like the coin in your home? During the "Crazy Period" of our parenting teens, Bobbi and I became so focused on the needs of several of our children that the other children felt neglected and became lost. Somewhere in our crisis we thought, "If we fail on this child, all the other children will fail too."

    How is your faithful child *really* doing? Who are his friends? What crisis is he facing? I know that one of our children faced a tremendous crisis, but because she thought, "Dad can't take any more," she kept her crisis secret. She became lost in her own home. She thought she wasn't loved in the same way, or that her needs weren't as important as the others'.

    Ask the Lord to help you see each of your children as individuals and ask Him to help you be used as His tool equally in the lives of all the children.

    Do each of your children know how you feel? How you love them? How you see God at work in their lives? Do you know their hopes and dreams?

    In the case of one of my daughters, she saw my concern for two of her siblings, and it took ten years of prayer and concentrated effort on my part to help her know I loved her equally. Ask the Lord to help you so that no one in your family gets lost, forgotten, neglected, or ignored. Go search for them!

3. Has your child, like a prodigal, chosen to leave your home? Act like the Heavenly Father **and let them go . . . but get your heart and home ready in hopes he'll turn and come home.** Read the story

of the prodigal son again. Learn from what the father did and *didn't* do. Is his example to you worth considering?

Caution:

Don't be paralyzed by the pain you feel over the prodigal in your life. If you don't find help and healing from God for your own heart and home, you won't be a changed person with a changed home for the prodigal to come home to! (Read chapter 15 for more on this topic.)

Turn your prodigal over to God. Perhaps you should pray, "Lord, please hit him with a brick! If I do it, I might choose a brick so small that I'd only make him more angry. If I pick up a brick too large, I might kill him! Lord, whatever it takes—even the loss of his health, wealth, or happiness—even the shortening of his life. Lord, whatever it takes, please bring my child to you." It's tough, but you can trust Him.

If your child is a Christian and has sinned against you or others in your family, practice Matthew 18:15-20.

▸ Go to him privately and "reprove" him, tell him the truth, and confront him with his sin. Offer to help restore him to God and then full fellowship with others.

▸ If he refuses to repent and be restored, take one or two with you and begin again. Is it time for you to take your mate with you? What about a close relative, leader from church, or Christian counselor? If he repents, help restore him.

▸ If he still refuses, tell it to the church. Tell the sin to the rest of your personal family, extended family, friends, and church family. Ask them to also go to your rebel—to confront and beg him to come home. If he repents, help restore him.

▸ If he refuses to repent, treat him like a non-Christian. Do not include him in your fellowship with other Christians. Don't ask for his prayers. Don't entrust your deep needs or secrets to him. Limit your fellowship with him in the same way you would to an unsaved neighbor.

If you can visualize where your child is in his "rebellion" and "return," it will help you know how to pray.

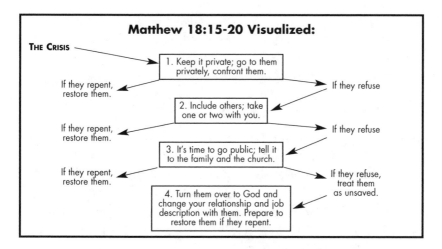

Matthew 18:15-20 Visualized:

THE CRISIS

1. Keep it private; go to them privately, confront them.

If they repent, restore them.

If they refuse

2. Include others; take one or two with you.

If they repent, restore them.

If they refuse

3. It's time to go public; tell it to the family and the church.

If they repent, restore them.

If they refuse, treat them as unsaved.

4. Turn them over to God and change your relationship and job description with them. Prepare to restore them if they repent.

4. Consider resigning. This can only be done with your adult children who are still living at home. I remember sitting with a brokenhearted parent whose efforts to deal with his eighteen-year-old rebel were creating a war zone in his home. He used the following letter to help establish peace in his home.

Dear _____ ,

We love you. This letter is our effort to help restore peace, so our home will no longer be a war zone. We believe you are just as tired of the conflict as we are, so we have decided that it's time for us to take the following course of action. We are resigning as your Daddy and Mommy (something we should have done a long time ago), and applying as your Dad and Mom and friend.

We have tried to provide for you: love, protection, guidance, oversight, discipline, a home, clothing, food, toys, transportation, car insurance, and other incidentals. Since God sent you into our home we have tried, the best we've known how, to assume the responsibility for raising you to love the Lord and become a mature adult.

The Reasons for Our Decision:

It appears to us that you have reached a place in your life where you believe you should be on your own, making your own decisions. You no longer respond lovingly to our efforts to provide guidance, discipline, and oversight. This is illustrated by the fact that you no longer want to obey the established rules of the home, and you no longer are acting in a respectful manner to us.

In resigning as Daddy and Mommy, we are giving you two weeks to decide whether you want to find somewhere else to live or whether you want to live in our home as adult daughter, friend, and partner. Please understand that this means we no longer will be obligated to provide for your needs. If there is a need, and we can help, we will if we think it a wise use of the monies and resources God gives us.

If you ask to stay in our home, you must respectfully agree to and comply with the following conditions:

1. *You must willingly treat us and speak to us with respect.*
2. *You must willingly keep the established rules of the house.*
3. *You must willingly agree to refrain from using profanity, from wearing suggestive clothing, using tobacco, drugs, or alcohol.*
4. *You must not have friends of the opposite sex in your bedroom.*
5. *You also cannot have your friends to our home in our absence without our permission.*
6. *You must willingly speak to your siblings with respect.*
7. *You must willingly keep an agreed upon curfew.*
8. *You must willingly partner with us in the work that needs to be done in the home.*
9. *If you are in school, you must attend school and maintain a passing grade and find a part-time job to care for your own expenses.*
10. *If you are not attending school, you will find and keep a job so you can pay an agreed-upon rent for living in our home.*

We love you; we didn't have you come into our lives to lose you. We know the constant conflict affects you as much as it does us. In many ways, you are more ready to be on your own and sometimes we aren't ready to let you go. We hope this step on our part will allow us to begin to live in love and peace.

If you choose not to stay in our home, we hope you know that we love you and that our prayer will be that the distance between us will bring us closer together.

We love you and are waiting for your response.

I started this chapter referring to the question asked me, "What should I do?" As I look back, I believe the only thing Bobbi and I did right was to not quit trying. They may be able to run from you, you may fail them, but please remember that God loves your children more than you do, and they can run from Him, but they cannot hide! In the middle of life's insanity, I hope this material helps you discover that our Father in Heaven wants every one of us to come home. If you are the prodigal, quit running and come home! If the train wreck of your life has destroyed your home, start over! If your rebel is still running, read the next chapter and allow God to help rebuild your heart and home for your prodigals to come home to.

Before We Married and Had Children

Our Expectations—Before we married, we thought our marriage and home would be a place where we would always be loved, admired, listened to, and respected. We thought our home would always be a place to run home to, a place of love and acceptance. That our home would not be just a house but a home—a place to flee to and not a place to flee from. A place where my wife and I would be partners and friends. We thought our children would come to us for answers and that we would always know how to counsel them.

And Then We Were Married and Then We Had Children.

Our dreams and answers turned to questions.

Written in My Journal during a Very Difficult Time:

Why would anyone want to be a parent? Why? When you don't have any answers that work? When everything you think and do is criticized. When everything you do, someone else's parent does better, or can buy their children more, or allows their children to do it differently?

Why? When every expression of love given to one child causes jealousy in the heart of another child? When you have to act like a parent in every situation even though you really want to act like a brat? When you have to sacrifice your money, your time, and your energy to provide for your children, but they get to spend any money they have on themselves?

Why? When no matter how much you do, how much you give, how much you sacrifice, it's never enough, never what they really wanted or expected.

Why? When they cry in the night out of fear or depression and you are expected to understand, to encourage, to reassure them? And who do you call on when you are afraid and need encouragement anyway?

Why? When you provide for presents and extras for your

children, but there is seldom a thank you, and certainly never a gift in return for you.

Why? When everything you do, someone else's parent or teacher or friend has a better idea? When everything you say could have been said in a better way?

Why? When you have to give up the things you want to do, to do the things that need to be done so you will have a healthy family, but no one ever notices what you are doing or what you have sacrificed.

Why? When you take some desperately needed time for rest and recreation and someone resents the fact that you weren't there when they needed you?

Why? When you go to the children to address their need, brokenness, and failure, and then you are strongly criticized for your own needs, brokenness, and failures?

Why? When conflicts break out in the home and you have to be the one who seeks forgiveness, or forgives first, or is big enough "to put it behind you"?

Why? When you offer your love to your children and they want everyone else's love but yours?

WRITTEN AFTER I TOOK MY EMPTY HEART TO THE LORD:

Why? Because in the bearing and raising of children, we learn to love others just like God loves us. Because your children will see God's love in you and may want to be like Him. Because some day, they may turn out to be your best friends, and the love you gave them when they were young will come back doubled when you are old.

Why? Because even if they never see or accept your love, Jesus, the one who loves you unconditionally and completely, asked you to.

Thank you for reading this chapter.
Dad/Grandpa/Friend

CHAPTER FIFTEEN

What to Do While the Rebel in Your Life Is Still Running

I don't know how you are handling your situation, but when our prodigals were still running, I was a bundle of contradictions. One moment I wanted them to come home, and the other moment I was afraid they would. One moment I was looking for more answers, things to try, and the next moment I wanted to resign and quit! Whether your rebel is a mate or a child, the ones left to rebuild wear themselves out trying to keep the rebel at home, fix what's broken, or control the damage to themselves and the rest of the family. The result of our efforts looked more like a shipwreck than a home. Everyone was drowning.

Shipwrecked!

Most shipwrecked marriages and families I've known had been sailing fairly smoothly until a massive storm threw them off course and into the rocks. Life's storms or tragedies come in all different forms. No matter the visible cause of your shipwreck, when you or those you love are at risk you want to do something!

Can you picture them floundering in the water, crying for help, afraid they are all going to drown?

I can remember the hurting husband in one broken relationship, the wounded wife in another, and the struggling parents in yet another. How painful it was to watch their loved one crying out for "Someone—Anyone!" to help. They were good people who wanted so badly to help. When they pleaded with their mate or child, "Take my hand, I'll help!" they were refused.

This week I sat with another shipwrecked husband. His marriage was sinking. One minute his reaction included angry threats and the next, he was ready to do anything to "fix" his marriage. Nevertheless, his desperate appeals to his wife fell on deaf ears. So, why is that?

I think it's because the drowning family member looks over to their willing mate or parents, and realizes that they are drowning too! They are smart enough to know that if they reach out for the willing family member, they will all drown. And so, taking their eyes off of the willing family member, they search desperately for anything that might keep them afloat—if only for a while.

Surviving the Storm

In the middle of a family disaster most people go through the process of denial, blaming others, and feeling numb.

- Some people try to survive by turning to alcohol, only to find the tragedy is still there when they sober up—and now they may have more problems.

- Some try to mask their pain with drugs, but again, the pain is still there when the effect of the drugs wear off.

- Some give in to depression. In their loss and grief over the broken relationships, they withdraw into themselves. They may ultimately consider taking their own lives.

- Some give themselves over to guilt. They dwell on what they wish they had or hadn't done. They live their lives with the regret of "If I'd have only," "I should have," and "I could have." They torment themselves with the absolute belief that if they had only been a better spouse, parent, son or daughter, sister, nephew, friend, preacher, policeman, teacher, etc., this wouldn't have happened. Somehow, we all feel as if there is something more we should have done.

- Some live in constant fear, worry, and even nightmares because the tragedy is yet to be resolved. They don't know how it will "turn out," and they don't feel safe.

- Some obsess with finding an explanation for the rebellion. This search for answers from the past steals their future.

- Some are so overcome with hurt and anger that rage begins to control their lives.

- Some are plagued with doubt. Someone may say, "God will take care of the children and they will be OK," but we think of other children who never came home.

- Some may become bitter and hardened. Someone might say, "I understand," but bitterly we think, "No they don't!"
- Some look for new relationships hoping to be rescued.

What Can We Do to Help?

Some people, trying to help, make the mistake of giving pat or inadequate answers. Some may think they're offering encouragement saying, "God is in control," but instead leave the hurt wondering, "Then why did He do this?" Some may try to help and say, "God cares." But it rings hollow for those who are left wondering, "If He cares, why did He allow this to happen?" Some, looking at the broken family may assume, "They must have done something to deserve this," and others will quickly think, "No matter what they did, no one deserves this!" Usually people don't know what to do or say.

I have struggled too. What hope can I give this brokenhearted husband? What help can I offer the wife of a rebel husband, or the parents of a rebel child? Better yet, what can *we* do while *our* rebel is still running? What can *we* do when *our* home is shipwrecked?

It seems to me that no matter whether it is a husband reaching out to his wife, a wife to her husband, or parents to their children, there are at least three choices they can make in their effort to keep from drowning themselves.

You Choose

1. **You can choose to take all the blame.**
   Will you concentrate on the areas of failure in your life and feel like "It's all my fault"? Will you become overwhelmed by your our own guilt, feel like you have to run after the rebel in your life and you become a doormat and a beggar? Whatever it takes to bring him or her back?

2. **You can choose to judge.**
   Will you concentrate on their failures, concluding, "It's all their fault"? Will you withdraw from them, becoming angry, demanding, critical, and defensive?

3. **You can choose to trust.**
   As I sat this morning with that wounded husband, I tried to help him picture his family floundering in the water so that he would understand that his only hope was to personally

cry out to the Lord for help. There's not a lot he can control, but he can make decisions for himself. He can trust the Lord to get him to the shore, and with the Lord's help be ready, when his rebel looks to him for help. He can prepare himself, with Jesus' help, to throw the rebel a life preserver when he is finally ready.

Getting Ready

What will happen when your prodigal quits running and looks to you for help? Will you still be treading water, trying not to drown? Or will you be ready?

Bobbi and I, our family shipwrecked, clung to God and each other while the ship of our family was sinking. We determined no matter our feelings of guilt or anger, we wanted to look to the Lord and let Him rebuild us into a home for our children to come home to.

I am grateful we had each other through those rough times. When one of us wanted to quit, the other looked to the Lord and helped the other to hold on.

Little by little we took the steps we needed to prepare ourselves and our home. We asked the Lord and our family to forgive us for our past. We couldn't go back and make it brand new, remove their memories of our failures, but we could ask the Lord to change our lives and begin to rebuild our hearts and home. We asked the Lord to help us heal and become a different family. If we had not healed as individuals and as a couple, our home would not have continued. There would not have been a home for our prodigals to come home to when they were ready! And when they wouldn't let us rescue them, we asked the Lord to raise up other people to help rescue them.

Instead of just waiting for our rebels to come home, we decided to practice the new things we were learning, and we tried to help others keep from making the mistakes we had made. We had to relearn how to love, forgive, and have healthier relationships so we would do a better job . . . if our prodigals came home. And they did!

God Brings Healing

I'm so glad God gives us second and third and fiftieth opportunities to get it right. Take another look at how God *rebuilds* relationships. How He can help you do a better job with the rest of your children, a new mate, your grandchildren, new friends, and other people's children. Your own home may be rubble, but God wants to remove the rubble and rebuild a heart and a home to come home to!

As we look back to the shipwreck of our home and we see what God has done to bring healing, we are so grateful. For so many years we lived without much hope, just trying to be faithful. I wasn't sure that we would ever see our hopes for a healthy home come true. I'm so glad that God forgives, restores, rebuilds, and allows us to start all over again. Our daughter Joni spent much of her first 28 years feeling nothing but hurt when she thought of our home. Step by step, healing and restoration has helped her replace the hurt memories of her childhood. For years I lived, almost without hope that she would see the changes God has made in our home so she could truly come home to our hearts. On our 35th anniversary she wrote to us and I could see that finally she saw, not just what we were, but what God is making us to be. She wrote:

A Home for Wayward Hearts

For twenty-eight years I watched my parents work and provide for our family. I've watched them struggle to put food on their table and clothing on their children. They struggled to pay for medical costs and housing. They will never be able to retire, and they do not own their own home.

Even with all they have been unable to provide for their children or themselves, they are the richest people I've ever known. They trusted in their Lord to provide for them, and they worked together to do His bidding. Hundreds of people have temporarily resided with my parents. Thousands of people have been fed. Their home and hearts have always been open to anyone who had need. They touched people's lives in a way that few can. They befriended the friendless, provided hope for the hopeless. Their home is a home for wayward hearts, hearts needing love, hope, and joy. While living under my parents' roof, they taught us to be unselfish, giving people. They taught us to share our hearts and reach out to those around us. Their lives will be remembered by all who know them.

They do not leave a legacy behind them in dollars and cents. They leave behind them a legacy of love. A legacy of joy. Those who know them well, those who have found shelter for a time, those who found an open heart and an open door whenever needed, will never forget them.

They followed their Lord, paid the price He asked, and looked only to the hour, allowing God to provide for their needs. My father is ambitious to reach out to every community with a new church. Eager to help, my mother, blindly, it always seemed to me, trusted the Lord she loved to take care of her. Whenever they go from us, we will not *forget the life they have led. Not always right, not perfect, but always growing, always teaching, and always respected. Last but not least, always an open door for the lonely, unloved, hopeless, faithless, friends. Always a home for any of us with wayward hearts.*

Written by *Joni Foreman*

Her love for us and her forgiveness to us is helping her see what God is rebuilding us to be!

Right Thinking

There were so many things that raced through my mind when my rebels were running. There were many nights when I lay awake trying to leave my burdens with the Lord. It was especially important to have "right thinking" as I asked the Lord to prepare my heart and home for the prodigal's return—as I tried to recover from "the shipwreck." John 14 is my favorite chapter of Scripture and has brought me a lot of peace and comfort—as well as "right thinking."

When I am upset:
> [1]*"Let not your heart be troubled . . . believe in God, believe also in Me."*

When I think about dying.
> [2]*"In My Father's house are many dwelling places, if it were not so I would have told you; for I go to prepare a place for you;* [3]*And if I go and prepare a place for you, I will come again, and receive you to Myself; that where I am, there you may be also."*

When I am confused about which way to go
> [6]*"I am the Way."*

When I don't know what is true and what is false
> [6]*"I am the Truth."*

When I feel all shriveled up and dying
> [6]*"I am the Life."*

When I struggle to believe
> [11]*Believe me because I said it! . . . "Believe Me that I am in the Father and the Father is in Me."*

When my faith in words is gone
> [11]*Believe Me because I did it! . . . "Believe on account of the works themselves."*

When I feel like my life will never amount to anything
> [12]*"Truly, truly, I say to you, he who believes in Me, the works that I do shall he do also; greater works than these shall he do; because I go to the Father."*

When I need a reason beyond myself for my choices or actions
> *[13] "Whatever you ask in My name, that will I do, that the Father may be glorified in the Son."*

When I get all caught up in doing things for Him instead of doing things with Him
> *[15] "If you love Me, you will keep my commandments."*

When I am running on empty and feel powerless to go on
> *[16] "And I will ask the Father, and He will give you another Helper that He may be with you forever; [17] that is the Spirit of truth, whom the world cannot receive, because it does not behold Him or know Him, but you know Him because He abides with you, and will be in you."*

When I feel alone, like an orphan
> *[18] "I will not leave you as orphans; I will come to you."*

When I feel like He is far away
> *[21] "He who has My commandments and keeps them; he it is who loves Me; and he who loves Me shall be loved by My Father, and I will love him, and will disclose myself to Him."*

When I want Him to live with me
> *[23] Jesus answered and said to him, "If anyone loves Me he will keep My word; and My Father will love him and We will come to him, and make Our abode with him."*

When I'm not sure who is my true friend
> *[24] "He who does not love Me does not keep My words; and the word which you hear is not Mine, but the Father's who sent Me."*

When my load is too heavy
> *[26] "A Helper, the Holy Spirit, whom the Father will send in my Name."*

When I can't remember
> *[26] "He will teach you all things and bring to your remembrance all that I said to you."*

When I feel trouble inside of me or around me
> *[27] "Peace I leave with you, My peace I give to you; not as the world gives do I give to you. Let not your heart be troubled, nor let it be fearful."*

Are you shipwrecked? Going down? Look up!

Dear Family and Friends,

Divorce hurts!

As I write today about divorce and the damage it causes, it makes me think of my aunt. I only have good memories of her. She brought joy and humor to all our family gatherings and I love her. Because she meant so much to me as a child, I have tried to keep her in my life as an adult.

When my aunt and uncle divorced forty years ago, it was because my uncle didn't know the Lord and his ungodly choices and actions destroyed his marriage and family. When they divorced, she and the children not only lost a husband and father, but they also lost their grandparents and extended family they had gained by the marriage.

His choices hurt everyone, but really damaged my aunt and the two children most.

Even though people let my aunt down, God never quit reaching out to help her find healing. He brought her a new husband who loves her, and her children and grandchildren and friends adore her, but the open wounds and scars of divorce still remain.

Why am I thinking about her today? When I write about divorce, I understand why God hates divorce. Remember He loves the divorced! Over the last years I've watched God reach out and restore my uncle first to himself and then to his children. He and his new wife (our dear friend) helped us start a church and I watched him be sorry for his past, come to trust in Christ, and then try to build a future. I watched him ask forgiveness and try to make restitution for his past. I've watched the Lord bring his daughter and son back into his life. I'm proud of him.

Before he died, I remember receiving a call from my aunt and hearing her say, "Last week he (my uncle) called me and asked me to forgive him." I asked, "What did you tell him?" She said, "I told him 'No' and hung up." She paused and said, "But yesterday I looked up his number and called him back and told him I forgive him." Just days later he died and we gathered together, not to remember the choices of his past, but the last years of his life when he was allowing the Lord to use him to bring healing.

The choices that lead us to divorce—when we break trust with God and our family—leave either open wounds or scars for a lifetime. But no matter our choices, the Lord chooses to keep offering to forgive and help us to be restored to those we've hurt.

Thanks for reading,
Dad/Grandpa/Bill

CHAPTER SIXTEEN

If You Divorce . . .

(The Chapter I Hope You Never Use)

Please don't take a permanent solution to a temporary problem. Don't rush into marriage, into having children, into the death of your marriage, or into taking your own life.

Divorce. It isn't what God wanted. It's not what you thought would ever happen, but now that it's here, what can you do?

We talked again last night. Her husband has slipped out of fellowship with God, chosen to leave her, and has compromised his example to his family and friends. We talked about her scriptural right to divorce and go on with her life (Matt 5:32). We talked about her emotions. One moment she wanted to run after him and beg him to come home no matter what, and the next, she wanted nothing more to do with him because it just hurt too much! In those moments, she just wanted to get a divorce and get the terrible waiting over. She said, "Almost none of my friends are calling, I don't know whether they don't care or if they just don't know what to say. *Bill, what should I do?*"

If you are separated or are considering a divorce, read chapter 11. If you are already divorced, keep reading! You're not alone, and there's hope even in your circumstances.

How Does God Feel about Divorce?

God hates divorce. Malachi 2:16 says, *"'I hate divorce,' says the Lord, the God of Israel."* He hates divorce because of the hurtful consequences of broken hearts, homes, and children. It hurts those He loves, often separating them from Himself and His eternal purpose for them. I have come to the conclusion that God hates divorce for *any* reason. It is a painful illustration of someone not trusting Him or not allowing Him to help them with their hurts. For that reason, anything short of the total commitment of the total person for the total life is a miscarriage of what God desires marriage to be.

How Does God Feel about Me?

One man sat in my office and said, "I've broken my promise to be faithful to my wife and we are now divorced. Do you think God still loves me?" He was so filled with guilt for his choices, broken promises and dreams, his immorality and divorce that he felt abandoned by God. Were his feelings true? Has his immorality and divorce separated him from God? If so, is that separation permanent? Is there any hope for his being restored to God and to his family? Even if his marriage is over and there is no possibility of restoration, can he marry again?

I believe sin, any sin, separates us from God, ourselves, and others. I believe God loves even those condemned to hell, but unless they turn from their sin and accept God's forgiveness and healing, their lives, families, and future will be filled with pain.

How does this affect those who divorce? I believe God hates divorce but loves the divorced people. I believe God hates divorce because it causes such pain to the people He loves.

Divorce Raises So Many Questions

What damage will this divorce cause to my children?

No matter who has the majority of the blame in your failed marriage, the death of love, trust, intimacy, and relationship leaves everyone wounded, but especially the children. You can't control how they'll handle their own pain or make decisions for their hearts, but you can model a healthy relationship with God. Let God heal you so your children can have at least one parent who shows them how Christians act and how God brings healing. The good news is that God can take our messes and make something beautiful—if we let Him. He's in the business of using broken people to do great things for His kingdom. Divorce will hurt them, but they are not ruined. God has a plan for their lives too! Let me suggest you *not* start with trying to restore your relationship with your children, or those you've let down. Start with being restored to the Lord, and as you heal, you may not be able to be restored as husband/wife or parent, but you can move from being the enemy to being a brother or sister in Christ. I know in my life, I fouled up being daddy, but God and my children's forgiveness has given me a chance to be restored into their lives as dad, as friend, as brother in Christ.

What about how you deal with people who are critical of you?

Sometimes those we most need the help from, seem to let us down when we need their support the most. If you come from a family where few divorces have occurred, you may struggle even more. There may be someone in your life who wrongly believes that "if you only did right," "followed God's instruction," "tried a little harder," "loved them with the right kind of love," "had gone to church," or "had been a better Christian," you would still be married. These aren't bad things, but it takes two people trying to make a marriage thrive. Being around them may make it harder for you to heal. If you and your family are broken, please remember the only one you can make choices for is you. And you can choose to let the Lord heal and forgive you. God wants to use you to forgive and heal your broken relationships. I've learned to "listen" to everyone who wants to give me advice, thank them for their love and concern, and then "do" what I believe God wants me to do. If you overreact to their counsel, you may be cutting off people you will need most in the future.

Why are my friends ignoring me?

I've noticed that whenever there is a fight, friends and family often choose up sides. Some friends may encourage you to be bitter and blame your "ex" for all the problems. Some will encourage you to protect yourself and try to get as much of the "spoils of the marriage" as possible. Some friends will encourage you to start "looking for love in all the wrong places," but most friends don't know what to do or say. Many say and do nothing. I suggest you find someone who loves the Lord more than they love you, but who really wants God's best in your life, and ask him or her help you walk with God through this crisis.

Am I a loser?

It's easy to blame others for the first few broken relationships, but you may now be asking yourself, "Why do I keep choosing losers?" or concluding, "Maybe I'm the loser." If your life seems to be a series of hurts, let me suggest that hurt people form hurt relationships. If two hurt people are drawn to each other with the false hope that "maybe this time," or, "this is finally the one." They will only be hurt again.

Can I suggest that you stop looking for "Mr. or Mrs. Right," and let the Lord bring health and healing to you as a person? I would suggest that until you heal, and until you find someone whom God is healing, you will only get hurt again. Stop where you are! Let the Lord heal you! Let the Lord help you discover what godly relationships are, and then let Him be the matchmaker by bringing a vibrant and healed Christian into your life. I want you to understand that until there is forgiveness and healing for your own sins and healing and forgiveness for the sins of others, you will remain hurt. What you will bring into the next relationship is hurt not health, and you will form another broken relationship.

Please consider going back to the beginning of the book and start over as a person before you try to start over as a partner!

Will I have to be alone the rest of my life?

If you have been asking other people whether you can ever remarry, you will be so confused by all the varied answers.

I remember a wonderful friend who had been married, separated, and then divorced from another dear friend of mine. I watched them both try to be healthy and have a healthy marriage, but all they did was create more and more hurt.

After more than 10 years of trying to restore his marriage, he met and fell in love with a lovely Christian woman and wanted to be married again. He sent letters to those he loved and respected and asked them to counsel him on whether he should remarry.

- Most of his friends didn't know what to say, so they said nothing.
- Some of his friends quoted Scriptures that said he couldn't remarry as long as she was alive or until she had committed adultery.
- A few of his friends asked him about his walk with the Lord and whether he was controlling his sexual desires—and if not, it would be "better for him to marry than to burn."
- Two of his friends said they would withdraw their friendship with him if he remarried.

What do we know? God's desire for us to marry "until death do us part." Moses "allowed" divorce and remarriage because of the hardness of the Israelite's hearts. They weren't allowing the Lord to work in them to bring forgiveness and healing.

- We know that the death of our mate allows us to remarry.
- We know that if our mate commits *porneia*, which is Greek for any sexual sin, and breaks our covenant with God, we are free to marry.
- We know if we are married to a non-Christian, and he or she refus-

es to accept us as Christians and he or she leaves, abandons, forsakes us, we are "free to remarry, but only in the Lord."

Confusing, isn't it?

- We know that all sin has consequences. Have you sought restoration of the broken marriage by forgiving and asking forgiveness? If restoration is not possible, are you asking God to love that person through you as a fellow Christian? If not as a Christian, as a neighbor? If not as a neighbor, as an enemy? Are you being used by the Lord to help the children or others in your life to also forgive? Are you asking the Lord to help you set appropriate boundaries?

How Can You Move Beyond the Hurts?

What do you do now? Well if you are my kid, whether you or your mate were immoral, gave up too soon, or just couldn't try anymore, you call me and I'll come take you home. I don't mean I'll take you to my house (I might do that too), but I'll be there to take you to your Heavenly Father. Your hurts and questions will go far beyond what I can "fix" or answer, but God is ready to begin the process of restoring your heart and your life. No matter who is innocent or guilty, everyone close to you will be hurt—everyone will need God's help and healing.

I believe that divorce, like any sin, can be forgiven, but no matter who is at fault, no matter who quit, no matter the circumstances, there are consequences for every sin, and it seems with divorce, it will be the children who will pay the highest price for the decisions their parents make.

Begin the Process of Healing

1. Understand your own part of the problem. If your mate is 80% to blame, God still holds you 100% responsible for your 20%. You can't make choices for your mate, but you can make choices for yourself. Ask the Lord to help you see your own part in your failed marriage. If He reveals sin in your life, take responsibility, humble yourself before God, and ask Him to forgive you. Commit to learning and growing so those mistakes won't happen again.

2. No matter the reason for the broken marriage, who wanted to quit, or how much pain you feel, don't hide from God. The Lord is available to you. You are important to Him and you can trust

Him to get you through. Read 1 Peter 2:19-25. Take your brokenness to the Lord and ask Him to help you. Maybe you need to ask God to help your belief become faith, and your fear to become trust. Commit your ways to the Lord and put your trust in Him (Isa 26:3).

3. Understand that this crisis will damage you, but it need not take your spiritual and emotional life. One woman said, "It helped me to remember that in the end, I will have to stand before God by myself and give account for my actions. I won't be blamed for others' choices." Once we get right before God, Jesus wants to restore us. If you struggle with hopelessness and depression, read chapters five and eight.

4. It's okay to hurt. Don't try to stifle the pain and act "strong." Statements like, "I'm glad my spouse is gone," "I don't miss him or her at all," and "I really don't care," really tell others more about the quality of love you were *not* giving your spouse than about how well you're adjusting to his or her absence or rejection.

5. If your "heart is broken," it doesn't mean you are destroyed. One part of you is broken, but you are not worthless, unwanted, or ruined. If your marriage has ended, I hope you *feel* completely broken. But please take a look at your whole life. The sum total of "You" is not just your broken marriage. There is more to your life—more to "You!" Like someone with a rebellious child or a parent with dementia, you grieve the loss (or deterioration) of an important relationship. But "You" is made up of many relationships that God wants to use to help you. Let me illustrate:

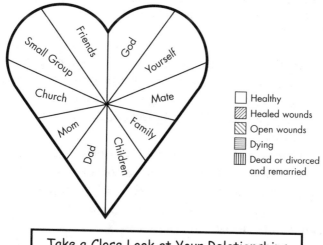

- ☐ Healthy
- ▨ Healed wounds
- ◩ Open wounds
- ▤ Dying
- ▥ Dead or divorced and remarried

Take a Close Look at Your Relationships

If your physical heart was diseased or had a blockage, the doctor would take the time to examine you thoroughly and then do whatever is necessary to protect your life and help you return to a happy, productive life. Take the time to examine your other relationships. Recognize their importance, and ask the Lord to help you strengthen the relationships that remain.

6. Have you forgiven those who have wronged or abandoned you? Forgive them from your heart, and turn the one who hurt you over to the Lord for judgment. Read chapter four for more on forgiving others.

7. Is it *you* who failed? Have you forgiven yourself? Ask the Lord to forgive you and help you seek forgiveness and restoration from those you failed. Read chapter three if you need help forgiving yourself.

8. Have you sought godly counsel? Be careful who you receive counsel from. Ungodly advice will encourage you to nurture bitterness, strike back, and take that person for all you can. Keep being faithful to the Lord, His Word, and His Church. Measure all counsel against the Scriptures.

9. Remember that as long as there is life and Jesus, there is hope. Attend divorce recovery classes and read Christian books that relate to your circumstances. Get professional Christian counseling if you need it. Pursue any possibility of rebuilding your marriage. Don't damage the possibility of your marriage being healed by starting to date.

Even If Everyone in Your World Lets You Down, You Are Not Alone

If, for whatever reason, you feel alone, know that God is with you. Paul wrote in 2 Timothy 4:16-18, *"The first time I was brought before the judge, no one was with me. Everyone had abandoned me. I hope it will not be counted against them. But the Lord stood with me and gave me strength."* Jesus promises to His followers, in John 14:18, *"I will not leave you as orphans; I come to you."*

I'm sorry God's best for you didn't work out because of the choices you or those in your life have made. God still loves you and is waiting to help you through this crisis and to heal your hurts. He still can take broken lives and marriages and fix them. The question is, "Are we willing to let Him?" Tough stuff.

God loves you and so do I.

A closing letter to my children and grandchildren and friends,

When I started this book I wanted to leave you a legacy of "golden nuggets" I've been given through the years. I wanted to be sure nothing got in the way of telling you how much I love you, but there is one more thing I want you to know. I'm really looking forward to meeting the Lord . . . face to face. I've seen Him by faith, but I've never seen Him with my eyes, heard Him with my ears, or touched Him with my hands.

Have you ever wished the Lord would step out of a picture or physically step out of the Bible and be real to you? Are there times in your relationship with Him when He seems more like an all-powerful creator who's busy somewhere else? Has He seemed like a distant relative you visit once in a while but really don't know? How many times have you prayed that He would be a Father to you, that somehow you could hear Him call your name, and that you could climb into his lap and feel safe? I understand.

When I was three years old, my dad was serving in World War II, and my mom and I were living with my grandparents. I'm told that every night my mom would put me to bed and go downstairs and cry. Often, I'd want a drink of water, and then I'd have to go to the bathroom. Finally, I would cry, and my mom would climb the stairs to find me holding the picture of my Daddy in his sailor suit. She'd enter the room and I'd sob, "I want Daddy to come out of the picture and kiss me goodnight." Because my mom wanted the same thing, she would cry with me. Sometimes I feel that way about my Heavenly Father.

When the Lord calls me home, please let me go. Don't hold on to me. Don't try the medical miracles to keep me alive. If He calls me home, I can then be really alive for the first time in my life. It's then that I'll get to bow down before my Heavenly Father, hear His voice, look into His eyes and say, "Thank you. I love You!" I'll get to see my grandparents, my mom, and others whose lives have been used to help me along my path. Before I meet my Bible heroes or see my precious friends who've reached heaven first, I want to sit down with my physical dad. Because all the reasons we couldn't talk will be gone, and I'll be able to say "I love you. I'm glad you were my dad." I'll get to hear him say the words I've longed to hear, "I love you too, Son, and I'm proud of you."

Kids, you can be sure, I love you and am proud of you, too.

Thanks for reading,
Dad/Grandpa/Bill

CHAPTER SEVENTEEN

What I Want to Be Like When I Grow Up

Keep On Dreaming!

When I dream, I dream young men's dreams. When I plan, I plan a young man's plans. But then I look in the mirror. There I stand in all my glory: white hair, bifocals. My body is the temple of the Holy Spirit; I just put a large fellowship hall in the middle. My teeth are mine; I bought and paid for them! When I look at my medicine box, I realize all those pills are probably what's keeping me going. I take a pill for this and a pill for that, and my medicine bill each month is like the national debt! In addition to that I have sleep apnea, and I sleep with a machine. But me old?

One day I sat down and thought about some of the most influential people in my life and their effect on the people around them. They inspired me. I've set my hope on someday becoming a general in the Lord's army. Think about it:

The General's Greatest Battle

(Quiet. Don't disturb him; the general is leading in battle.)

When he was young, the army of King Jesus gave the fresh recruit his armor, helmet, and a shining sword. The boy became a man with armor scarred by many battles. He learned to lead by following. With many battles fought and won, they made him a captain of warriors. His speeches rallied the people, his thoughts were quoted, and his name was mentioned with honor and respect. But he is no longer a Captain, he has been promoted to a general in the war!

His living place is now a small apartment. He has outlived most of those who cheered his name. This one-time giant now seems so small.

His once powerful voice is now a whisper. His exploits have been forgotten by all but a few on this side of heaven. But wait! There is movement!

In the quiet of the night, in the middle of the morning or in the middle of the day . . . there it is! The general and his wife move to take down their armor. It's so scarred with the marks of battle, but they lift their battered swords once again. They lead the young recruits, the warriors, the captains into battle as they pray.

➤ *They know the fears of being new recruits who are unsure of how to fight.*

➤ *They know the warriors' temptations to take credit for themselves.*

➤ *They know the burden of being captain in King Jesus' army. They know how difficult it is to care for the army and still look to the needs of their own family.*

➤ *They have watched so many fall in the middle of the battle.*

➤ *They know the inner struggles and fears, the loneliness, and the sleepless nights leaders in the Lord's army face.*

So they pray. And when they pray, they fight their greatest battles and win their greatest victories.

(Quiet now . . . Listen!)

The general and his wife are about to mention your name and mine to King Jesus!

Written by Bill Putman when thinking of:
Willie and Doris White, Elton Petrie, Fred and Carol Masteller,
Dick and Cay Ewing, and Walt and Helen Harris.

I have been a young recruit.

When I enlisted to fight, my Commander-in-Chief suited me with armor. He gave me the Bible, the Sword of the Spirit. King Jesus gave me the mission to rescue the perishing, to care for the dying, and to set the captive free. As I enlisted to fight, I enlisted in a war from which there can be no truce and no compromise with the enemy. As a young recruit I promised to pay any price, to go any place to engage the enemy, to pick up the fallen, to swing my weapon until my life breath was taken from my body and I fell in the middle of the battle. King Jesus gave me mentors to train me and to show me examples of what a Christian man and husband should be.

I have been a warrior.

As a young recruit, I yielded to the discipline, obeyed the commands and leapt into battle. My skills as a warrior increased, and captives were freed, wounded were helped, and battles were won and lost. I have thrilled to join with other warriors and recruits to penetrate enemy lines, to build beachheads from which to set captives free. My years as a warrior bonded me to those who shared my passion and fought in the battles with me.

I have been a captain.

As I faithfully served as a warrior, I was given the responsibility of being a captain. As a captain, I have led warriors and recruits. I have been assigned the task of speaking to the warriors and encouraging the recruits. I have helped strategize to recapturing every nation, state, city, town, and every man, woman, boy, and girl—for King Jesus. The passion for participating in Jesus' victory has consumed me. My years as a captain showed me the faithfulness of God to train me for service, to care for me when I was wounded, and to give me others to train.

I am now a trainer of leaders.

Two years ago I was called to work alongside our oldest child in a growing ministry. My ministry now is to be a mentor, a trainer of recruits, warriors, and captains. I miss leading into battle, but little by little, growing older is taking away my energy to do what my mind and heart still tell me I can do. In the not too distant future my energy will fail, my abilities will dim with my eyesight or my hearing. It's then, that I pray God will allow me to become a general.

Why do I want to live long enough to become a spiritual general?

I've noticed in my life that the new recruits take my time, warriors thrill my heart, and captains challenge my commitment, but it's been the few spiritual generals I've known who have had the greatest effect upon my life. These generals have been close enough to God to mention my name in prayer, and close enough to me to give me godly counsel.

- I recall Elton, who became a general in spite of serving from a wheelchair for 60 years. He, my childhood Sunday School teacher, prayed for me every day until God called him home.
- I think of my grandparents, Elmer and Esther, who loved and prayed for me as a child and believed in me as an adult.
- I treasure my friends and mentors, Fred and Carol. Although Fred's health broke when he was in his late 50s, I've watched him

accomplish more by prayer since then, than when he was in active ministry. Other than Bobbi, no one on earth has been used more to help me.

- I think of my mentor and counselor, Dick, who just went home to heaven. His health and memory failed, but he prayed every day for the Lord's new recruits, warriors, captains—and for me. At the end of his days, he hardly remembered anyone, but when I called he would say, "Is this my son Bill? I'm praying for you."
- I think of Dean. His life challenges me onward, and his phone calls remind me that I am in his prayers.
- I think of George, who taught me so much in the classroom, but whose greatest lesson was how to die.
- I think of Walt and Helen, who let me borrow them as parents when my own died. I know they pray for me every day.
- I think of Willie and Doris. Willie's life challenged me to give my life to church planting. God used Doris to call me back to Him when I was 20.

Sometimes I look back and long for the excitement of the battle and wish I were young again. Sometimes I am restless and discontented with my role of mentor and trainer. Sometimes I am almost jealous of the captains who lead and speak. But when I get quiet before the Lord, and I look at those who have had the most lasting effect upon my life, I look forward to the day when I'll be promoted to general!

How do people become generals?

You can't become a general without being a recruit. You can't know the needs of the warriors and captains without having been in the middle of the battle. Generals become qualified for the job when all their personal resources are gone and they have to totally depend on the Lord.

How will you know when you are ready to be a general?

- ➤ When your energy is failing and your recollection of the day *you* were recruited is but a distant memory, but you pray faithfully for the Lord's recruits.
- ➤ When your warrior days are long gone, and even though you feel a bit disconnected from the battlefield, you pray faithfully for the Lord's soldiers.

➤ When, no longer able to carry the pressures and burdens of a captain—leading the army into the battle, seeking to destroy strongholds, standing against false arguments, pulling down obstacles, and taking every thought captive—you still stand to cheer for the warriors and pray for them faithfully.

➤ When experience and age make you more effective in the classroom than the battlefield, training up the leaders of tomorrow . . . and you continue to pray.

➤ When poor health slows you down, but now, with fewer distractions, you have time to put an arm around the young warrior, pick up the wounded, and grow closer to the Lord through prayer.

➤ When the number of your birthdays or the medicines you take limit the ways you can share with your wife, but together you are young again when you take down your armor and pray for all the young soldiers of the King.

➤ When your mate no longer remembers you, or disease has stolen his or her strength, but together, with nothing else to offer, you give the Lord your faithfulness and pray.

➤ When your mate dies or your world becomes silent with the shroud of deafness, or darkened by blindness and you continue to pray.

➤ When you are weak, old, and alone, but still with your heart in the battlefield, you pray.

➤ When you are dying, and you ask the Lord only for the strength to say one last goodbye to your children and grandchildren before at last you pass with the triumphant shout of "**Jesus!**" on your lips.

    . . . You might be a general!

The Key: Don't Give Up . . . Look Up!

If the battle of your life is longer than you expected, don't be one of those who wastes his nights and days with regret. Set in your mind the hope that after your ability to do or say is gone, you will be given the high privilege of being one of the generals in the Lord's Army—spending your last days and last breaths lifting up the names and needs of God's people to Him in prayer. To the blind eye, you may appear useless, but what is more powerful than prayer?

Consider the apostle Paul in Philippians 1:12-26. He was imprisoned, facing the uncertainty of life and death. People had pushed him out of leadership and were taking his place. He faced tremendous inner conflict. He had come to the place where it would be better for him to die and be with Jesus; he was locked away, removed from active ministry, limited in his ability to preach, and unable to mentor. He wanted to pass on, to be with the Lord, but he also felt the need to stay and fight with His people. Paul determined to ask the Lord for strength to "stay on," and God used him in a mighty way—writing and praying!

Instead of "stepping down" from being the captain of the army, the leader of the battle and greatest missionary of all time, he could step up to become a great general through prayer!

My Hopes and Dreams

My dad's health broke at age 62, and he died at age 73. My grandfathers died at 87 and 93. What about me? Only the Lord knows. Will health issues limit my ministry or shorten my life? I don't know, but I am dreaming dreams and making plans to still be ministering in some way when I'm 91. Why 91? I'm aiming for 91 because that's how old I'll be when my house is paid for. I'm aiming for 91 because at 63 there is still just too much of "myself," "I," "me," "my," and "mine" left. I still need weeded and matured.

I'm trusting and praying, that as the things I can do or think or manage are slowly taken away, and as I slowly spend more time *with God* than doing things *for Him*, my most important ministry will be just beginning as I devote myself to prayer. I'm aiming at 91 because I can visualize myself as one of those few older people who have a joy in living and a love for children! I want to be an old man who is great to be around because he brings love and encouragement to others.

What Will My Future Hold?

If I am in a wheelchair in the nursing home, I can roll myself into each room daily, "calling on my flock," reminding them that Jesus loves them, and encouraging them that "the best is yet to come!" Even if my eyesight is gone, I can still quote Scripture to my little flock.

If my voice is gone, my family could make copies of my favorite Scriptures for me—to give away. If I'm stuck in my bed and cannot leave my room, I could still *be* a sermon of kindness and patience to everyone who enters my room.

Think of it. No matter the past, the number of times we fell down or were wounded in the battle, or the limitations of our talent or health, when all the above has passed us by, we can still do the most important job in the Lord's army. We can pray!

I want the last of my life to weed out human distractions so I can become like my friend, Willie White. From the nursing home that is now his solitary existence, deaf, bound to the bed or chair, no longer a recruit, a soldier, or a captain, he has become a general in the Lord's army.

Facing the End

I said to my son Jim some months ago, "I'm going to live long enough to be a burden to my children." He jokingly replied, "Well, Dad, you can die any time then." But seriously, when it is my turn to face the coming end of my life, I want my little bed to be a temple, not be a prison. I want my lingering life to be a blessing, not a burden. Though I am sure I will long to be with Jesus, may I determine, like Paul, to "press on" as long as He would have me stay. By faith and by the strength I know the Lord will offer me, I can picture myself lying in my bed taking down my battered armor, picking up the Sword of the Spirit, which is the Word of God, lifting you up to Jesus, and cheering you on in your battle.

Closing Thoughts

Most twenty-one-year-old's dreams don't come true.

Going through some old papers I found a poem I'd written when I was just 21 years of age. I had just returned to the Lord and He had started reforming my dreams for my future. Before understanding my purpose for living, before finding Bobbi to share my life, before children, or any of the adventures of my life I wrote this poem.

The Bells of Heaven Rang
In a room that was filled with glowing
Of the sun burning the darkness away,
An old man lay quietly dying,
For his life was ending that day.

In his heart he could still remember
The joys that had filled his life;
Of the youthful days of laughing
And the blessings of children and wife.

He remembered joys of Christian living
And the blessings of serving the Lord,
Of the ones he'd helped to Jesus
And the treasures in Heaven he'd stored.

As the light there seemed to grow dimmer
And to him seemed to fade away,
He knew he would soon see Jesus
And see Christ smile that day.

With the thrill of soon gaining glory
Yet with quavering voice he asked
To hear softly "Rock of Ages,"
For he knew his time was past.

With the triumph of going to heaven
Yet tearfully his loved ones sang
As his soul winged its way to Jesus
And the bells of heaven rang;

"Rock of ages, cleft for me,
Let me hide myself in Thee."
Bill Putman, June 1963

As I reread my poem written at age 21, I thought "I could be called to the Lord today and it's all come true!"

What's next in my adventure? Whether it is when I'm 63 or 91 and it's my turn to go be with Jesus, my last breath here will become my first breath in heaven. I will then join with God's people of all the ages and sing praises to our Savior and be prepared to shout with victory when you finally end your battle and get home to heaven.

Growing older but believing "the best is yet to come!"

Still wanting one more giant to fight and one more mountain to climb,

Dad/Grandpa/Bill